Hemingway
in CUBA

Hemingway
in CUBA

Text
Gérard de Cortanze

Photographs
Jean-Bernard Naudin

Éditions du Chêne

Contents

Foreword 7

The Sun Also Rises Over Havana 9

Ngaje Ngái or The House of the God Beneath the Trees 57

Beyond the Great Blue River 101

Hemingway: Guía General 147

Bibliography 165

Appendices 166

In one of his letters, Hemingway wrote that as far as he knew, he had only
one life to live, and wanted to live it where he chose. He added that he
had found a marvelous place to go to: Cuba.

(*selected Letters*)

Foreword

A book rarely flows forth from the pen of the writer fully-armed. It has to mature, wait, disappear, come back again no one knows quite why or how. I discovered Havana and Hemingway at the same time, while I was preparing an edition about Latin American literature, with Julio Cortazar, Regis Debray, Saul Yurkievich and the members of the Group called *Change*, a review that was launched in Cuba in 1968. This was a long time ago, and yet it seems like yesterday. Almost thirty years have passed. Since then, Hemingway and Havana have never left me. Each in their own way. Hemingway intermittently, and Cuba more steadily, through publishing, translation, reading and friendship. This book is a gesture of friendship towards my Cuban friends who have taught me so much. Severo Sarduy, who gave me Barroco dancing and initiated me into the mysteries of Eliseo Diego and Portocarrero; José Lezama Lima who allowed me to plunge into the sacred water of the Dador; Guido Llinas who, in a far off suburb light years away from Guanabacoa, gifted to me the black signs of *santeria*; Eduardo Manet who taught me clear-sighted nostalgia; Ramon Alejandro and his fierce machinery; Guillermo Cabrera Infante, whose Orbis Oscillantis I published. All of them were at my side, in Jaimanitas and in the calle Obispo, on the Prado and the Rampa, on the steps leading to the terrace at the *Finca Vigía* and the steps leading down to the *jai-alai*. A silent crowd of guardian angels, at the window of Ambos Mundos and in front of the façade of the former *Embajada Norteamericana*, in the streets of Barrio de San Isidro and under the statue of San Antonio Abad, accompanied by his pig, at Regla. All of them, including old father Duick, the Breton fisherman from my childhood who took me fishing along the *Côte Sauvage*, in the halflight of dawn, where, while I watched them rowing, sitting at the back of the boat, I felt "completely certain I would never die".

Gérard de Cortanze

The Sun Also Rises Over Havana.

I have often wondered what I should do with the rest of my life and now I know – I shall try and reach Cuba.

ERNEST HEMINGWAY
To Pauline Hemingway, at sea, around March 28, 1928, *Selected Letters.*

rnest Hemingway occasionally spoke about the trilogy he was writing on "the land, the sea and the air." Perhaps the least sedentary of his creed, for a number of years Hemingway nonetheless found his *terra firma* in Cuba, that "home from home" he always came back to from no matter where. Even as a traveler, he was an adventurer, never shying away from danger. He was fascinated by Cuba, and enveloped himself in its atmosphere. In his books he evoked the smells of the streets and the mills, the warehouses and molasses, the alcohol, the sugar cane juice used for rum making, fuel, the whiff of fried food, sweat, and the aroma of roasting coffee that was more powerful than the actual drink. Those delicate and ephemeral fragrances of tobacco. Then there were stenches that scared the birds searching for mangoes. Vulgar, obscene odors. The smell of the distant plantations. The smell of traveling and dust. Smells of branches and palm trees swishing in the northerly breeze. The smell of subtropical winter days. Odors wafting across from the nearby port, Casablanca, La Regla, the smells of the Bay of Havana, and of the sea, where, in a heavy swell, "steering was like riding a horse downhill" (*Islands in the Stream*). For Hemingway, Cuba begins with Havana, and with that "sea looking hard and new and blue" (*To Have and Have Not*), that is the sea of Key West.

At the westernmost point of Florida, surrounded by treacherous shipping waters, shallows, isolated reefs, currents and cyclones, lies Key West. An island

On his way back from France in April 1928, Ernest Hemingway cruised on board the Steamship *Orita* just off Havana.

covered with flowering shrubs, coconut palms, pepper plants, tamarind trees, guava, Key West was to become the home port that would enable this modern day St George to slay his inner dragons. Hemingway had a strong passion for steamers, and crossed the Atlantic by ship a good thirty times, at one point making four crossings in one year, and was, throughout his life, in search of a mooring, a place of his own. His friend John Dos Passos had enthused about the string of islands stretching south from off the coast of the Florida peninsula and about one of them in particular, *Cayo Hueso*, Key West: He described it as a coal port linked by ferry to Havana, with merchant ships anchoring in the dock. The smell of the Gulf Stream hung in the air. The cigar factories had attracted a population there that was half Spanish, half Cuban.

On his return from France in 1928, in the company of his second wife Pauline Pfeiffer, after an 18-day crossing between La Rochelle and Havana on board the Orita, Hemingway got the urge to explore this "dream country", so often praised by his dear friend Dos. Key West was an island a mile wide and five long and at the time had a population of around twelve thousand. Only ninety miles to the East of Havana, separated from the island by the Florida Straits and the Gulf Stream, it could be reached by ferry. Here, in what he called the poor man's St Tropez, Hemingway had his first taste of Cuba. On the main street of Key West, he found Cuban cafés, Havana brothels, a bar that was as dark as it was sordid: Sloppy Joe's. In the adjacent, half-paved streets, stood rows of old white houses, all with front porches and verandas, giving them a vaguely "New England" look. He immediately fell in love with the place. Here, the humid air was laden with salt, and the trade winds blowing from the Atlantic brought occasional short spells of coolness. Carlos Baker, in *Hemingway, A Life Story*, described the way Hemingway "set off straight away to explore the island and its banks of yellow seaweed, the jellyfish beached on the southern shore, the closed down boatyards and little Spanish restaurants. Ernest loved to watch the continual to-ing and fro-ing: cargo ships, yachts from Florida and the big gray coastguard patrol boats prowling round about the peaceful old port that used to be the haunt of pirates such as Henry Morgan." Throughout the twelve years he spent here, working intensely, Hemingway rubbed shoulders with millionaires, fishermen, sailors and many other friendly, suspect, ordinary or eccentric characters, who supplied him with the raw material for his fiction.

One of the fundamental reasons for moving to Key West was his need to come back to the States, after having been so far away. Initially, he took up temporary residence, and then bought a charming house, at 907 Whitehead Street. Born in 1899, Hemingway was like a tired hero, affected by the First World War, in which he had been actively involved. He was seriously injured in July 1918 near the village of Fossalta, on the *Piave*. He was more European than either Dos Passos or Faulkner who, two or three years older than Hemingway, were not really part of the same generation – due to the war they were not able to take part in. Hemingway was violently opposed to an American society with which he never ceased to settle the scores. He had been to hell and back, and paid very dearly – with two hundred and twenty-seven pieces of shrapnel in his right leg – for the privilege of being if not conscious, at least clear-minded. So dearly that he preferred fleeing and denial. While Dos Passos was writing *USA* or *Manhattan Transfer*, books full of industrialization and sky-scrapers, social problems and the struggle for survival, Hemingway, in the forty-nine stories that comprise *The Nick Adams Stories*, was drawing a picture of bucolic, provincial, eternal America, full of rolling plains and meandering rivers. But it would be wrong to oppose the rural nonchalance of the young Nick to the struggles of his contemporaries, who, at the same time, were fighting for child labor laws. Hemingway found his best defense against nothingness, his struggle against the angel and all "lyrical illusions", in his solitary work as a writer. John Brown was right to say that all his activities – hunting, fishing, bullfights, drinking – couldn't prevent him from hearing the roar of the world. (*Hemingway*).

The fact is that at Key West, Hemingway distanced himself from American society. He fled a nation shaken by prohibition, in the throes of the Depression. Unlike Faulkner, whose character was formed by his roots in the Deep South, he refused to identify with the land of his birth. With the exception of a few short stories, it is strange to note the almost total absence in Hemingway's work of the American West and the Hollywood phenomenon, of which he was nonetheless a contemporary. His entire work takes place out-

Regla is the old quarter of Havana, situated on the other side of the bay. It dates back three centuries. Hemingway's yacht the *Pilar* was often to be found at anchor there.

side America: in France (*A Moveable Feast, The Garden of Eden*), Spain (*The Dangerous Summer, The Sun Also Rises, For Whom the Bell Tolls*), Italy (*Across the River and Into the Trees*), Cuba (*Islands in the Stream, To Have and Have Not, The Old Man and the Sea*). So there we have it: at Key West, Hemingway left behind his fixed image of the United States in favor of a country that he scarcely knew, Cuba, which was to become a real "refuge" for him.

This continual play between home and away, between distance and closeness is also evident in the choice of friends he invited to this place he considered paradise. John Charles Thomas, the opera singer; Canby and Esther Chambers, "a friendly and touching couple"; the Murphys and the MacLeishes; Max Perkins; the painters Waldo Pierce and Mike Strater; Evan Shipman, who became the tutor of his children. But other friends too, who had no connection whatsoever with the literary or cultural *milieu*. Short-lived or lasting friendships, struck up in bars or on the docks, during fishing trips or in fights and brawls: such as with Eddy Bra Saunders, a pirate on the Spanish boat *Valvanera*, who was the inspiration for a short story entitled "After the Storm," and introduced him to deep sea fishing. Jim Sullivan, the boat repairer... He forged a variety of sometimes unlikely friendships, with the idle rich, such as Charles Thomson. Disconcerting friendships that upset some of his closest friends, including novelist Marjorie Kinnan Rawlings, who reproached him for them in no uncertain terms. Friendship, that hidden sub-plot, a series of subtle wounds, an unbreachable contract made of mystery and silence, that Romain Rolland compares to an association based on mutual consent for talking about oneself to someone else; like the friendship between Hemingway and Joe Russell, the owner of Sloppy Joe's and former smuggler: "I used to be co-

Havana harbor seen from the district of Casablanca: Muelle de San Francisco, Muelle de Luz and Club Nauticó International.

owner of Sloppy Joe's" Ernest said "Silent partner, they call it. We had gambling in the back and that's where the real money was. But getting good dice-changers was difficult because if he was so good you couldn't detect it yourself, you couldn't know he wouldn't steal from you. The only big expense in a gambling operation is police protection. We paid 75 hundred dollars to elect a sheriff who, in his second year in office, went God-happy on us and closed us down, so we closed down the sheriff." (quoted by A. E. Hotchner, in *Papa Hemingway*).

But among Hemingway's friends, there was one who towered above them all, a possessive lover, an unfaithful mistress that he had to conquer, tame, subjugate and charm before he could land on the Cuban coast. That same coast that Columbus mistook for Cipangu: the sea. That ocean of a thousand faces that he ceaselessly explored just like the painter in Jorge Luis Borges who, having set out to draw the world, peopling his advancing years with a diversity of images, realizes just before his death that his "painstaking labyrinth of shapes" was nothing other than his own self-portrait.

First of all, *les cayos*, the Islands in the Stream, bits of broken land, a hyphen, at the extremity of Florida, between the civilized continent of the United States and the primitive continent where the magical forces of nature and man can deploy their full potential, where the writer seeks the refuge necessary to work, away from inopportune visits and telephone calls.

Habana Vieja seen from the rooftops of the Seville-Biltmore Hotel.

DOUBLE PAGE FOLLOWING: Founded on July 25, 1514, Havana became a freeport in 1818.

Cayos with long, white beaches edged with coconut palms. The fishing trips always started with a trip out into the middle of the reefs, along the channels, and continued with a journey among petrol fumes, on board borrowed or hired boats, with the slow, steady vibrating sound of a large Palmer engine. The directions and destinations varied. Along the Marquesas islands, from where Waldo Pierce brought back a six foot long tarpon; the area around Bimini, where, after an interminable crossing, the exploit consisted in pulling a giant tuna fish onto the boat whole, before the sharks tore it to shreds; around the barrier reef that extends from Florida over a hundred and twenty miles and leads to the sun-baked Dry Tortugas.

Listed as a Worldwide Heritage site by Unesco, the old town constitutes an exceptionally rich blend of Hispanic American architecture in Colonial, baroque, neoclassical and art deco styles or, as depicted here, monumental railway and industrial buildings.

How many times Hemingway must have sailed up the Calda channel, that wild serpent that cuts its way to the east and the west of the main northwest channel, to spill into the Gulf of Florida? Key Largo, Upper Matecumbe Key, Vaca Key, Sombrero Key, Looe Key, Key West... Behind: the bay of Florida; in front: the Florida straits and Cuba. Hemingway escaped, set off in pursuit of that shining greyhound of the seas, the wahoo, of green and yellow hued dolphins, pilgrims that could wrench the line and the reel from you in one incredible run, tiburons, *sábalos* and *lisas francesas*. To reach Cuba, Hemingway followed the Gulf Stream, that great river, thirty miles wide and six hundred fathoms deep. He entered the Gulf Stream at a point in the Bahamas, between Tennessee Reef and Muertos Keys, at a point where the color of the water changes from shimmeringly clear white near the fine sandy beach, to green, to aquamarine, and he only has to follow the timeless deep blue of this unique stream that runs all the way from the Sargasso Sea to England.

Hemingway quickly got to know Havana, through friends and fishing. With men and the sea. One night, on his way back to Key West from one of their trips, when they had just dined on shellfish soup and fried amberjacks seasoned with a concoction based on brine and sweet lime, all liberally washed down with Bacardi rum, their boat came alongside a key situated on the opposite side of the Morro lighthouse. On board, along with Ernest, were Arnold Gingrich, future owner of Esquire, and Dos Passos. This was in 1929. The rest was nothing but one long return journey between Havana and Key West. In 1932, Hemingway went dragnet fishing (using mackerel as bait) along the coast of Cuba. The first time he stayed for ten days, then, deciding to postpone a trip to Africa in favor of a second fishing trip to Cuba, he stayed sixty-five days.

Havana Harbor seen from
Casablanca. February 7, 1959.

During this second trip he caught sixty-two swordfish, and, as he wrote in a letter to Guy Hickock, on October 14, 1932, he learnt a lot about Cuba. He returned several times in 1933, on board the '*Anita*', Joe Russell's boat. Ernest and Joe went beyond *La Corriente* to fish in the waters of Havana. They stopped off to rest at Cojimar, Mariel and Bahia Honda, sheltered ports that became their operation bases. They got hooks from the local fishermen, listened to the advice of these men who knew the waters like the back of their hand, observed the depths, the habits of the fish and the company they kept. In 1934, after he had bought himself a boat, the '*Pilar*', in the spring-time, Hemingway left everything to return to Havana by the first ferry, which docked at Ensenada de Atarés:

the fisherman of the village of Casablanca, the fishing port of Havana, ensured that the starving marlins had put in an appearance and that they caught an average of fifty a day!

From then on, Hemingway used Havana as subject matter. As early as April 1933, he planned a long fishing expedition to Cuba, not only to practice the sport he loved, but also to gather material about the Gulf Stream. He was planning a long short story that would be set in Key West, Havana and the sea separating them. His hero was to be called Henry – the name of the infamous pirate Morgan – and would have the personality of Joe Russell. Havana gradually provided Hemingway with a number of romanesque experiences, including some brushes with trouble with

FOLLOWING DOUBLE PAGE: *Habana Vieja*. The sea towards the Gulf of Mexico

Cuban pirates from La Regla district, the poorest area of the whole port, from the spring of 1936. In his book, *Hemingway, My Brother*, Leicester Hemingway related that Ernest made friends among all the pilots in the port Association, but he couldn't very well gain the sympathy of all the smugglers, garbage men and bandits who roamed round the port in their boats or motorboats on the lookout for craft that were badly guarded by their crews... That spring, rumor had it that an instruction had been given in Havana: the first person who could take the Pilar would win the honors of the whole of the Regla quarter.

While he was writing a series of articles about fishing for marlin off the Morro for Esquire magazine, and finishing the second part of the story of Harry Morgan, *The Tradesman's Return*, and 'In Blue Waters', a piece which formed the basis for *The Old Man and*

Capitolio Nacional Guía provincial de la Habana, 1944 Copied from the Capitol in Washington, it was inaugurated in 1929 and today houses the Felipe-Poey Museum of Natural History.

the Sea, Havana gradually loomed larger in his imagination. Havana and *le Malecón*, that long, deserted avenue where the wind full of saltpeter whipped the arcades of worn, damp stone. Havana and the first May rains beating down on the road, whipping up the smell of damp street while in the distance sailed a fleet of cargo ships and sparkling American automobiles sped past. Havana, the main character in *To Have and Have Not*, with the dome of the Capitol and the hotel Nacional, and the Morro lighthouse, a halo of lights facing those of Rincón and Baracoa. Finally, Hemingway's own Havana was born, the one he observed: the old town, *La Habana Vieja*, with its Gothic and Moorish convolutions, its parthenons and formidable Renaissance dust, the smell of printing and cooking, entablatures, sickly columns, faint glowing lights from another era, the stench of malangas and bougainvilleas, the crowded, voracious, bustling streets. A Havana that was all confusion, all in scrolls (volutes), patios and terraces, a mixture of neoclassical, baroque and colonial architecture. A fat, asthmatic Havana. A Havana full of smoky shadows and lanterns. Hemingway – an American in Cuba. What did this child of the Midwest make of all these Corinthian acanthus, pedestals, urns and vases, and moldings, the agony of the façades and arches? What did he make of the fluting, the cornices, this man who narrowly escaped death in Italy and lived in Key West?

Opposite the fountain of the *Indienne du Paseo de Marti*, he stared at the ineffable white marble. On the Pradó, he watched young girls, dancers, processions and celebrations on Sunday evenings. Granite had not yet replaced the ornate mosaic paving and the multipurpose window, adopted from New Orleans and called "French window", had not yet been replaced by the heavy shutters of "Miami" windows. Havana was opulent then. You only have to look at the advertise-

Le Malecón. Several miles long, this boulevard runs from the fortress of San Salvador de la Punta as far as the Tower of Chorrera.

ments produced at the time, *pieles, joyas, vestidos,* boasting of the delicatessens, shops selling clothes, luxury goods, decoration, furniture, cosmetics, perfumes, jewelry. As far as American banks were concerned, the capital boasted eleven of them!

To come back to the lights of the town, which Gabriel García Márquez considered the most beautiful city in the world at that time, and which Hemingway first saw from the sea, like Santiago, in *The Old Man and the Sea,* fighting an enemy he can hear and feel rather than see, and that has just bumped against the keel of his boat: "The reflected glare of the lights of the city were only perceptible at first as the light is in the sky before the moon rises. Then they were steady to see across the ocean, which was rough now with the increasing breeze. He steered inside of the glow and he thought that now, soon he must hit the edge of the stream."

Havana, ever-present Havana. The Havana of the naval dockyard, where Richard Gordon, in *To Have and Have Not,* believes the coastguard is anchored. The Havana of the stone and brick building of the First State Trust & Savings Bank. Of the San Francisco wharf where Harry takes his boat. The Havana of the San Isidro quarter and Jésus Maria. Of the Plaza de la Fuente, the fumes from the Companía de Electricidad and Castillo de Atarés where Colonel Clittenden was shot. The Havana of O'Reilly Street, Optica Lastra, no. 506, where Hemingway bought his spectacles. Of the café La Perla and the Cunard bar on the *muelle de*

Le Paseo Marti, also called the Pradó. At the turn of the century this large street linking the Central Park and the Malecón was lined by magnificent neo-colonial villas.

come from the background of an American childhood with a repressed father and a domineering mother, after running away a first time to Paris, a second time to Key West, he chose to run for the third time at the end of 1939, by moving permanently to Cuba. Havana is far removed from that artificially disinfected world, for a variety of complex reasons.

Beyond the humid nights, the fragrance of a hothouse full of wilting flowers, of the busy or deserted streets of *La Habana Vieja*, its arches, its benches, its grocery stores, its eloquent storytellers, there are the bars, stifling when there is no air conditioning, draping the shoulders with a cape of coolness when there is. There was Ciro's, which Hemingway frequented from time to time. Rancho's, the famous restaurant with a terrace, which also served as a brothel and Chinese Opium den. The Casa Recalt, opposite the Ambos Mundos, between Cuba and San Ignacio – purveyor of Hatuey beer and supplier to the *Finca*. Sloppy Joe's, Zulueta 252, situated not far from Sevilla-Biltmore and not to be confused with the one in Key West. And there were others, the haunts of prostitutes like "Honest Lil" in *Islands in the Stream*, standing out against "panama hats, Cuban faces and the dice cups shaken by the customers."

San Francisco. The Havana of the Centro Vasco and the Zaragonzana (one of the best Cuban restaurants in the 1940s, a stone's throw from El Floridita) where Hemingway used to run up a tab. That of the Cuartel de San Ambrosio, of the *muelle de la Luz* and the Club Nauticó Internacional. The Havana of the old Palacio de los Deportes where Hemingway was presented with the *San Cristobal de La Habana* Medal in 1956. That of the Agencia 4-10-06, the branch of the Banco Nacional de Cuba, at 420 calle Amistad, where Mary Welsh, scarcely a week after her husband's suicide, in July 1961, came to retrieve the manuscripts of *Islands in the Stream* and *Moveable Feast*, as well as the unpublished stories of Nick Adams and the draft of *The Garden of Eden* from the strong box.

Which Havana did he see, that American who originated from a puritan culture that he took so much pleasure in denouncing? The unconventional American that he was, irksome, in rebellion against the inertia of a society lost in self-satisfaction. He who had

However, the most important bar was no doubt the Florida, which everyone called the Floridita. At that time, there were no framed photographs showing Hemingway with Gary Cooper and Errol Flynn, Mario Marcia Menocal and Robert Herrera were not displayed on the walls, the tourists did not ask for a Papa Doble. As A. E. Hotchner recounts: "At that time the Florida (that was its proper name but everyone called it the Floridita) was a well lighted old fashioned bar restaurant with ceiling fans, informal waiters and three musicians who wandered around or sat at a table near the bar. The bar was massive, burni-

La Plaza Vieja. The Art Noveau
hotel built on this site was
one of the most prestigeous
in Havana in the 17th and
18th centuries.

FOLLOWING DOUBLE PAGE:
Old Havana. The rooftop
of the cathedral. The Morro
Lighthouse can be seen
in the background to the
right of the picture.

Cathedral Plaza, north of the Plaza de Armas. Built in the 18th century by the Jesuits, it was long believed to be the resting place of the skeletal remains of Christopher Columbus.

shed mahogany: the bar stools were high and comfortable, and the bartenders cheerful, skilled veterans who produced a variety of frozen daiquiris of rare quality." (*Papa Hemingway*). The rest, or should I say, the legend, Hemingway entering the sacred premises, stocky build, muscular arms, wide, white sports shirt floating over his khaki trousers, brown moccasins worn with no socks, has become a part of false literary history and its fantasies – more than its ghosts. No, decidedly, the original Floridita was a place of friendship and it is the one in calle Obispo, on the corner with Bélgica (Montserrate). The Floridita is the place where records were broken and challenges met; a place where provocations were rife, the type of provocation that makes people feel they exist when they feel life is passing them by, when the need for recognition is such that only surpassing yourself can reassure you that you really exist. Hemingway recounts his drinking exploits in a letter, remembering a day in 1942 when he was grounded because the weather was too bad to stay out on the sea, and he met up with Guillermo, the Basque pelot player, at the Floridita. It was around half past ten in the morning and Guillermo had been playing the day before and lost and Hemingway was exhausted. They both drank seventeen iced double daiquiris that day without leaving the bar, except to go occasio-

nally to relieve themselves. Each double contained 4 ounces of rum. That makes 68 ounces of rum. But there was no sugar in the daiquiris and they both ate two steak sandwiches. Finally Guillermo left to go and referee a match that evening. Hemingway drank one more double then went home and read all night.

The Floridita: a place where fights broke out and trouble was common, at the end of the descent into the beating heart of *Habana Vieja*. It was also a place for meetings, some of which failed to take place, like the meeting arranged by journalist Kenneth Tynan between Hemingway and Tennessee Williams. The meeting between the "extrovert and the introvert", the "songster of action" and the "disillusioned analyst", the two extremes in American literature, was a "memorable failure" (*Defense of the Realm*). The Floridita, a place where jokes were bandied for the entertainment of all, like the Royal Order of Shrimp Eaters founded by Hemingway – the members had to eat the heads and tails. In *Islands in the Stream*, Thomas Hudson, under the eye of the "bandits' navy or coastguard", got drunk at the Floridita with Cuban politicians who had dropped in for a quick drink, but also with the old, respectable prostitutes with whom all the regulars had slept at one time or another in their life; with sugar cane planters; civil servants drin-

The Floridita. Corner of the famous bar frequented by Hemingway. His barstool.

king in their lunch break; with under secretaries and assistant undersecretaries from the embassy; with the inevitable friendly FBI agents and all those so keen to look like young, irreproachable Americans that they made themselves conspicuous as surely as if they had been wearing their Bureau badge on the shoulder of their cotton suits.

The second place was the hotel Ambos Mundos, which he discovered in April 1932. A modest hotel, that was not included in the guides at the time along with the list of those recommended for American tourists – such as the Sevilla-Biltmore, the Almendares, the Inglaterra, or the Florida, located in the same street as the Ambos Mundos. Like the Floridita, it is situated in calle Obispo, but at the other end, on the corner with Mercaderes, only a few yards from the Plaza de Armas where one of the imposing façades of the United States Embassy could be seen. In the nineteen thirties, calle Obispo, with O'Reilly street which ran parallel to it and San Rafael street, was one of the busiest shopping areas in Havana. There were up market shops that welcomed customers in several languages, luxury printers, banks, travel agents, fashion stores and boutiques as well as an extraordinary book-

Hemingway at the Floridita with Gary Cooper.

shop, opened in 1898, called "La Poesía Moderna".

In the letter he sent to John Dos Passos, Hemingway wrote: "At this hotel – Ambos Mundos – you can get a good clean room with a bath right overlooking the harbor and the cathedral – see all the neck of the harbor and the sea for $2.00 – $2.50 for two people." (*Selected Letters.*) It was an ideal place to work. Behind the pink façade, between two sailing trips, Hemingway read the proofs for *Death in the Afternoon* (1932). In heat that was clearly reminiscent of the temperature in Piave in the summer of 1918, in room 525, he wrote a good part of A *Farewell to Arms*, as well as his first articles: "Marlin off the Morro" (Esquire, 1933) and "Out in the Gulf Stream"

(Esquire, 1934). From that window, to the left he could see the Colombus Cathedral and the rooftops of the Old Havana, directly in front of him was the harbor and, in the distance, Fort Morro and the Casablanca peninsula.

The English edition of *The Havana General Guide*, published in 1930, had an edifying foreword, set under a medallion of General Gerardo Machado, President of the Republicá, and specially written for North American visitors. It ran something like this: "The Island of Cuba, situated between the Gulf of Mexico and the seas south of America, enjoys a privileged geographic situation. With the gates of Havana closer than any other to our country, the Island of Cuba, enriched by considerable amounts of American capital attracted there by its marvelous natural resources and by the excellent conditions resulting from the recent Great War in Europe, presents, in our view, preponderant social and economic advantages. Its political status, ensured by the Platt amendment, nonetheless confers on it total political independence, materialized by a sovereign government, but in spite of this it is still, in a certain way, the natural prolongation of the coasts of America. Americans will find in Cuba a large number of their compatriots who play important roles in the fields of agriculture and trade, as well as sports and leisure activities they will feel perfectly at home with. Thus thousands of tourists from the United States have already chosen the Cuban coasts rather than the famous European capitals and pleasure ports." In *Hemingway, My Brother*, Leicester says of the Havana of the nineteen thirties that it was one of the most adorable, seedy, enchanting and strange cities in the whole world. He found Havana hospitable and full of Americans who willingly played host to visiting compatriots. This is a euphemism… The wind of madness blowing through Havana had

"When we went to the Floridita bar in those days [...] was just a nice bar where my father knew the staff and could drink with us and his friends." (Gregory H. Hemingway).

an underside. The hidden side, somber, black, economic, political, and human. Hemingway, who wrote *The Earnest Liberal's Lament* (1922), who called himself an individualist, which constituted nothing less than a sin to the Marxist critics of the time, ignored nothing of the exact situation of Cuba vis-à-vis its big American neighbor. Certainly, Paul Morand was able to note that Cuba was not in the throes of political and military disorder, in trouble over cars or money, which was the lot of Latin American anarchy. Certainly, American automobiles, with their roaring chromes, were tearing through Havana in all directions. Certainly, Havana was the empire for all forbidden games. But at what price! Since 1902, Cuba had

FOLLOWING DOUBLE PAGE:
The Floridita Bar. In the background, a view of Havana. "Honest Lil put her hand on his thigh and squeezed it and he was looking down the bar, away from Honest Lil, past the Panama hats, the Cuban faces, and the moving dice cups of the drinkers." (*Islands in the Stream*).

The Floridita. The best bar in the Carribean, according to Hemingway.

Drawing of the Floridita Bar published in Esquire in 1953, along with an article singing the praises of the bar as "an institution of integrity where man's spirits can be lifted by conversation and conviviality."

been a colony of the United States. Since the Platt amendment, which gave the United States the right to intervene in Cuba "whenever the social peace and security of American citizens was threatened", as well as the control of two military bases, Bahia Honda and Guantanamo, the Americans had used military intervention three times, in 1906, 1912 and 1917. From 1920 to 1933, while prohibition raged in the United States, the Republic of Cuba was a republic in name only. From 1925 to 1933, General Gerardo Machado led a reign of terror and corruption, and, according to Gabriel García Márquez, maintained a strange political cohabitation with the Chase National Bank and the Rockefellers. As for his successor, Ramón Grau San Martín, he was quickly ousted by Colonel Fulgencio Batista, who ended up leaving for the United States in 1944, only to return in March 1952.

At that time, American financiers and industrialists controlled 90% of the Cuban nickel mines and haciendas, 80% of public services, 50% of the railroads and, with the British, the entire oil industry. Hemingway was well aware of this situation. In *To*

Corner of Obispo, formerly one of the classiest streets in Havana. "This was the street he had walked down a thousand times in the daytime and in the night." (*Islands in the Stream*).

BELOW: Advertisement for one of the chic Boutiques on Obispo street, published in the General Guide to Havana in 1928.

Have and Have Not, the young revolutionary says to Harry: "You do not know how bad things are in Cuba. […] You can't know how bad they are. There is an absolutely murderous tyranny that extends over every village in the country. Three people cannot be together on the street." And in *No One Ever Dies*, a short story originally published in Cosmopolitan, in March 1939, Enrique and Maria, authentic Cuban revolutionaries, are assassinated by the police. The message of the story could not be clearer: Maria, before she dies under torture, says, that no-one dies for nothing. In Cuba, those who were initially considered to be heroes changed into veritable political gangsters, venal and ambitious. Havana turned into a land of incriminations and vendettas between rival gangs. Alejo Carpentier made use of this tragic situation to write *Manhunt*. In Havana in the 1930's, the prisons were full and a feeling of insecurity reigned throughout the island. The uprising in February 1935, during which government forces imprisoned and shot over three hundred people, heightened Hemingway's sadness.

He was not in Cuba at the time, but he had friends among the victims.

Blood was being spilt and fascism was raging. Langston Hughes, the famous African American poet, was turned away from a beach at Marianao, because of the color of his skin. Nicolas Guillén wrote in his memoirs (Actes Sud): "there was a huge scandal, but Langston was not allowed to swim on this beach or on any other beach on the island." To take up the expression of René Dumont, the United States took away from Cuba "the initiative for its own economic development", which did not prevent certain Cuban millionaires from having a short-lived field day in the nineteen twenties, known as the "dance of the millions." But here, more than ever before, nothing was simple and a superficial approach to all these interrelated events would serve no purpose. During a trip to Moscow in the nineteen thirties, Nicolas Guillén remarked: "What can people buy? The same things here as anywhere else; luxury coats or modest clothes, the same solid gold jewelry set with precious stones that are on display in the windows in calle San Rafael in Havana." The American presence was everywhere. In *The Old Man and the Sea*, Santiago talks about the time he spent in the restaurant La Terraza, in Cojímar; there he met John J. McGraw, who was just as interested in horse racing as in baseball. Billionaire Irénée Dupont de Nemours, the leading promoter of Varadero, bought part of the peninsula, and in 1928 had a palace built on the edge of the cliff at a cost of one million three hundred thousand dollars; the rest was sold in lots. Tourism slowly but surely became an important source of currency for Cuba. As for Colonel Fulgencio Batista, who was responsible for the assassination of Antonio Guiteras, the leader of the democratic opposition, he did not hesitate, many years later, in the middle of a world war, to have more or less secret dealings with fascist nazis – in *Hemingway en Cuba* Norberto Fuentes recounts the misadventures of Captain Ramirez, who sank a German submarine off the coast of Cuba only to be immediately disgraced: the honest military man was not aware of the fact that Batista was busy negotiating with Nazi Germany to sell them sugar and oil! – nor to exploit the collaboration that was objectively possible between certain elements of Stalinist communism and American capitalism, or even gangsters. Organized crime had never before flourished to such an extent in the island. Hemingway depicted this seedy, violent atmosphere in two of the short stories in the *Men Without Women* collection – *The Killers* and *Fifty Grand*.

American crime spread across the bay of Florida from Chicago and took up residence in Cuba. The charismatic Mafia leaders Lucky Luciano, Meyer Lansky and Frank Costello still live there. The Italiano family, who controlled liquor trafficking, owned a near monopoly on the *Bolita*, the Cuban lottery that is played by means of a hundred numbered balls. A whole network of moral and political depravity transformed the island into a pleasure center where, in a corrupt jungle, rich Americans rubbed shoulders with the worst criminals in the land. The police were a party to all this, as were the other public authorities. Almost all the gaming houses were in the hands of the gangsters, who were gaining ground, taking over the most legitimate government salons and enterprises such as hotels, bars, restaurants, dance halls, estate agents and the building trade. It was the gangsters' meddling in the hotel business that enabled the various gangs to set up their headquarters there and made Havana the winter capital of organized crime. In Havana, five major hotels were built by the Mafia: the Nacional, in 1934, the Deauville, the Comodoro, the Capri and the Havana Hilton. This is a classic busi-

PREVIOUS PAGE: Obispo Street
"This was one of the streets
he loved but he did not
like to walk along it in daylight
because the sidewalks were
too narrow and there was
too much traffic". (*Islands in
the Stream*).

OPPOSITE: The Hotel Ambos
Mundos. Between 1931 and
1936 Hemingway used to
meet the beautiful Jane Mason
here. After their affair had
ended, he described her as
"a damned bitch" in *To Have
and Have Not*.

ness scenario: clandestine bets are organized, casinos and cabarets opened (like the Sans-Souci); there is systematic corruption of the police and civil service. In Cuba, gangsters owned the casinos, part of the local telegraph agency, bookmakers' premises, companies operating coin machines and managed a network of white slave traders and pornographic cinemas. As for the gangster "elite", they regularly stayed at the Nacional, as "guests"of the management! In this way, Havana was not just leader in the drug trade, but also in clandestine betting and for the recruitment of hit men. For many years, Havana was literally infested by all kinds of gambling: bookmakers, one-armed bandits, lottery, dice games, poker, casino ships anchored offshore, etc. The profits amounted to millions of dol-

lars. Warring gangs kept the town in an atmosphere of latent violence that the State did not wish to dissipate, since it was a party to these seedy dealings. Wasn't it Lansky himself who was paid by the American State Department to ask Batista to give up the presidency in 1944? Wasn't it the same Lansky who went back to live in Cuba, in March 1952, just after the return of Batista? And before he finally left the island for good, after January 1st 1959, he had taken care to transfer the colossal fortune of the dictator to a foreign bank account.

But Havana was not only, as it was called at the time, the "*brothel of America*." During his visit to Havana, Spanish poet Federico García Lorca, who concentrated on the Havana nightlife and popular

Hotel Ambos Mundos.
The view from Room 525,
the room Hemingway always
stayed in. "At this hotel –
Ambos Mundos – you can get
a good clean room with a
bath right overlooking the
harbor and the cathedral –
see all the neck of the harbor
and the sea for $2.00 - $2.50
for two people." Letter to
Dos Passos, May 30, 1932.

The rooftops of Havana seen from The Hotel Ambos Mundos

haunts, admitted that he felt at home there, and praised the lifestyle that was "the color of rum". Guillermo Cabrera Infante evokes this strangely paradisiacal Cuba that you became attached to, where, in the pornographic cinemas in Barrio chino de Havana, certain films imported from Denmark or from the United States had provocative scenes added to them for the Cuban market, which had the reputation of being very hot! On the one hand, the "tragic decade", on the other hand, the "good life". Let's take a look at the good life first.

"This is the face I believed I had found again when I arrived in New York in 1980", writes Renaldo Arenas in *Avant la nuit* (*Before nightfall*) (Fayard); "The town sent me into raptures. I felt as if I had just arrived in Havana in its heyday, in the nineteen fifties, with wide pavements, fabulous theatres, a marvelously efficient transport system, with people of all kinds, with the mentality of a population that lives in the street, speaking every language; no, I never felt like an outsider in New York." This Havana of interminable nights is heavily scented with nostalgia, that Guillermo Cabrera Infante calls the "whore of a memory". Gabriel García Márquez comes as close as you can get to the reality of a town that became a sanctuary for pleasures when he describes the fact that there were

Letters received by Hemingway addressed to him at the Hotel Ambos Mundos. The room he stayed in has been turned into a museum.

La Bodeguita del medio, "where Hemingway drowned his innermost dragons in torrents of *mojito* cocktail." (Erik Orsenna, *Mésaventures du Paradis*, Le Seuil).

"even lotteries in the pharmacies, and aluminum automobiles too big for the colonial street corners" (*Autrement*, "Cuba"). To list the fashionable bars and nightclubs would make you dizzy. First of all, the Tropicana, of course, the most luxurious cabaret in the world, with its gold and silver curtains, its spicy heat and tropical glass dome roof. But there were also others: the Sierra, the Las Vegas, the Nacional, the Habana Yacht Club, the Casino Español, the Chori, Club 21, the San Francisco, the Carmen-Bar, the Cha-Cha-Cha-Club, the Saint-Michel, the Bar Celeste, the Cachot de Hernando, the Quick Lunch Bar, the Bar Humboldt, the Sky Club, the Maraka, the Kimbo, the Pigal, the Nocturno (on the site which today houses the Coppelia), with their climbing plants, fountains and multi-colored lights, and their half-naked women, and their international playboys, and their whiskies and their sodas, and their siesta, their poverty, their obscenity, their powdered singers. In Shanghai, displaying an advertising poster that announced a mysterious *Posiciones*, Graham Greene watched the lovema-

king of Superman with a little mulatto "with no great interest", lost money at roulette, smoked marijuana and watched Lesbian exhibitionism at the Blue Moon. In *Our Man in Havana*, Wormold lost himself in calle Lamparilla, the red light district, disappearing into the crowd of pimps and lottery ticket touts. In Havana, he said, sexual intercourse was not only the main commodity traded in the city, but it was also the entire *raison d'être* of the men. "It is bought or sold, it doesn't really matter which, but it is never given away." There were over seventy thousand prostitutes in Havana at that time. The government had found an honest façade behind which to hide a somewhat less than honest trade. It opened dance academies where the "dancers" enrolled. The very upright National Theatre even started up an annual competition in which the best dancers in the world at the time competed, but there was also a competitor called one Harry E. Guggenheim, United States Ambassador to Cuba... A rotten dancer he was really. What did it matter, when the head of State in person, Gerardo Machado, could manipulate the jury that awarded the prize to the American diplomat!

However, we may ask ourselves if the seedy, obscene, pornographic Havana of Graham Greene is the same Havana as the one Hemingway knew. Robert Escarpit was right to remind us that in *Father and Boy*, the answers the father gives to the young boy's questions about sexuality have a definitive sort of rigor, but also the brevity of a pedagogy that has no nuances. In fact, Hemingway probably had little to do with this permanently effervescent Havana. When he went to the Bar Basque or the Floridita it was simply to meet up with people, or he would go to the Stork Club, with Martha on his arm, when he wasn't holed up at the *Finca Vigía*. He would go fishing, pigeon shooting, he organized cock fights, went to watch jai-alai

La Bodeguita del medio.
"A dive full of aimiable scum,
near the cathedral, where
they serve *mojito* (a cocktail
made from rum, sugar, ice,
water and mint)." Jean-Francois
Fogel, *Autrement*, "Havana
1952-1962".

La Habana Vieja. Old Havana has been registered on the Unesco list of World Heritage sites since 1982.

matches at the Habana-Madrid Fronton, went to Vedado Tennis Club, played real-tennis with champions of Basque pelot such as Guillermo, Piston or the Ibarlucia brothers, or attended baseball matches, a sport which had pride of place in the popular culture of the island.

One haunting question remains: what did he really see of Cuba, this American who, as Erik Orsenna puts it, "drowned his innermost dragons in torrents of *mojito* cocktail?" Did he listen to Beny Moré, alias the mambo barbarian, then the barbarian of rhythm, and the liberated cadence of the *danzón,* to the sound of the bands of Orlando de la Rosa and Tito Guizar, Marío Fernández Porta and Pedro Vargas? Did he dance one of those frenetic rumbas, like the one called the donkey's kick, where the woman shakes her butt obscenely in front of a dancer who whips her rump with the corner of his handkerchief? Behind the false moustaches and false beards, the gunrunning and the noisy procession of corruption, gangsterism and debauchery for tourists, did he catch a glimpse of what made Havana for many years one of the musical capitals of America? In the nineteen fifties, the Blanquita theatre, which showed reviews and operettas, could hold an audience of 6,600. The press, with thirty different publications, played a crucial role in the life of current affairs in Havana. Then there was the radio — in 1944, in the Havana area alone, there were no fewer than fifty radio stations! — at a time when serials and musical programs, such as the one produced by Bacardi rum, occupied an important place. And soon there would be television... the cosmopolitan splendor of a town where some people could not see beyond the three hundred brothels also had an intense, indigenous cultural life, in spite of the gangsters and the repression. René Portocarrero and Amelia Pelaez created a Cuban baroque style in painting; Eliseo Diego celebrated the old avenues of Havana in poetry; some of the most subversive trends in artistic creation grew up around the Origenes group; theaters (Nacional

The former American Embassy building on the Plaza de Armas at the bottom of Obispo Street, a few yards from the Hotel Ambo Mundos. Thomas Hudson, in *Islands in the Stream* described the Embassy in caustic terms.

La Moderna Poesía. Now closed, La Moderna Poesía on Obispo Street was founded in 1885 and was the largest bookshop in Havana. Hemingway passed it every time he walked between the Hotel Ambos Mundos and the Floridita.

Palacio de Los Capitanes.
Situated on the Plaza de
Armas between Obispo and
O'Reilly, this late Baroque-style
palace was built in 1776,
when the plaza was rebuilt.
From 1902 till 1920 it
was the headquarters of
the Government of the
Island of Cuba.

Theatre, Payret-Theatre, Campoamor, Marti, Fausto, Rialto, Olimpic, etc.) and cinemas (Trianon, Riviere, Tosca, Majestic, Wilson) opened and prospered. José Rodriguez Feo, in his Letter to Havana, described the phenomenon: "The sustained development of art and literature throughout the nineteen fifties is one of the great paradoxes of our history. The crisis in our civil institutions, political and administrative corruption, the indifference of the majority of the population towards culture and the low level of official support for cultural creation did not prevent writers and artists from pursuing their creative production." (*Autrement*, "Cuba".)

This cultural development, which rested on illusory economic independence, had unexpected consequences in the field of architecture. If one particular district of Havana had to be associated with this period, it would obviously be Vedado, rich and famous since the nineteen twenties, especially around the calle 23 (La Rampa), which, in the nineteen fifties, saw the first Havana skyscrapers spring up, crushing with their presence the fragile tapestry of the shady streets running down to the *Malecón*. Havana in the nineteen fifties was a Havana that was changing its smell. The old buildings, which even today smell of gas and food – "If you found yourself in the street after six o'clock in the evening, you got the impression that the whole town was about to eat *picadillo* (minced beef)" (Gilberto Seguí) – were replaced by new ones that gave off the odor of acrylic paint and vinyl. The Fosca, the Someillàn, the building that houses the Medical pension fund, the Colina, the Havana Hilton, the St. Johns Casino all tower into the Havana sky. The Cerro baseball stadium was covered with a metallic structure; tunnels were planned under the river Almendares and the bay, which would enable Batista to build lucrative hotel chains and casinos on the eastern beaches. The

The Cuban-American mafia settled in Havana in the 1920's. It owned night clubs, cabarets and gaming rooms (opposite, the famous Bolita) but also several hotels and casinos. The advertisements reproduced here are taken from a Guía Social de La Habana published in 1959.

Cuban revolution, by drying up funds, put a stop to the ravages American concrete had started in Vedado. Havana is strangely enough today one of the few cities in the world that has been able to retain its unity or even its soul. In contrast to this Havana, an exact copy of a mini-Manhattan arrested in mid flight, witness of a utopic American way of life, of which *Habana Libre* still remains today the symbol, in contrast to the sky scrapers of the town that tower above us like "icebergs in the moonlight" (*Our Man in Havana*), José Lezama Lima opposes a more human city, one that is softer and "which is still able to be the golden section of rejoicing, the happy medium of grace, a response to a gentle caress."

Beyond Vedado and the delirium of Fifth Avenue Parkway (The Antillian Riviera) at Miramar, we find Hemingway's Havana once more, with nostalgia seeping from the crumbling arches, its columns and its colonial style that is Moorish in origin. Hemingway"s Havana, in which it is a sheer pleasure to drive around in a convertible along the *Malecón*, as in *Three Sad Tigers*, the novel by Guillermo Cabrera Infante: "This pleasure, this *joie de vivre*, the euphoria of the day at its best time, with the summer sun turning red over an indigo sea, amidst clouds that sometimes spoil everything by making the sky look like the sunset at the end of a religious film in glorious Technicolor, which didn't happen that particular day, even though sometimes the town is cream, amber and pink at the top while below the blue of the sea is darker, turns purple, violet, and starts going up the *Malecón* and penetrating into the streets, into the houses and only the pink concrete sky scrapers are left, creamy, almost the color of toasted marshmallows."

We have already mentioned what some Cubans have called the "tragic decade", which started at the beginning of the nineteen fifties. Hemingway, who had been married to Mary Welsh for four years, after a trip to Paris and to Venice, published *Across the River and Into the Trees*, in September. The book was slammed by the critics. Adriana Ivancich, the beautiful countess whose acquaintance he had made in Italy, came to visit him at the *Finca* in November. Stimulated by her presence, he began to write *The Old Man and the Sea*, which was published two years later, and, as we know, was very highly acclaimed. Luis Aguilar Leon was right when he wrote "at the beginning of the nineteen fifties, it would have been impossible to foresee the amplitude of the storm that was threatening Cuba. On the contrary, in January 1950, the Cubans had good reason to celebrate the New Year

The Vedado was full of these old villas that once belonged to rich Cubans or Americans. Some of the properties once used as casinos or *bordellos* today house schools.

in a confident atmosphere." (*Autrement*, "Havana 1952-1964"). However, the situation would deteriorate very quickly. The military coup organized by Fulgencio Batista against the government of Carlos Prío was no surprise to anyone, and what is more, did not even cause any immediate consternation, no doubt because the good citizens of Havana had had enough of the student protests and thought that this would bring an end to gang violence. But these years were black indeed. The government in power lied and cheated, just like their leader, who even played canasta surrounded by an army of servants to serve drinks and spy on the hands his adversaries were holding! While the dictator, who had an unhealthy passion for information, never began his day without reading intermi-

nable reports based on telephone tapping, the World's press thought everything was fine, and announced that peace was reigning in the island. And what a peace it was.

Riots broke out. During one of these riots, of the one hundred and sixty people arrested, sixty were killed after being tortured. In July 1953, Fidel Castro launched his famous assault on the Moncada barracks. The attack failed. He was released, along with his companions, in May 1955. Peace was not restored however. On the contrary, the opposition became more virulent: bombs went off, at both Santiago and Havana. The atmosphere on the island soon became noxious. In response to the growing activism of the opposition, nocturnal arrests and summary executions

Habana. Hotel Nacional.

The Hotel Nacional. Built by the Mafia, it was also a casino.

filled the country's daily headlines. In some ways, due to the town's geographic location, farther from the foyer of the rebellion, the Sierra Maestra, than Santiago de Cuba, Havana continued to live it up. The Tropicana was always full, and colossal amounts of money continued to change hands at the casinos. The Bodeguita del Medio, which had been enjoying renewed success since 1942, became *the* place for Hollywood stars to be seen in. And while the *fidelistas* were abducting the famous Argentine runner Juan Manuel Fangio, the Mafioso Meyer Lansky was shuttling back and forth between Washington and Havana.

Hemingway was not taken in. Living in San Francisco de Paula, ten miles from Havana, he was well aware that although fortunes were being spent at the roulette tables in the cities, horrible poverty reigned in the countryside: in 1958, fewer than three thousand landowners shared ownership of almost three quarters of the arable land. A hundred and forty thousand small farmers worked the remaining third and a hundred and twenty of these small properties were less than 50 acres in size. There was violence eve-

rywhere. Meyer Lansky, who, in 1946, had organized a magnificent reception in honor of Lucky Luciano, with special guest star Frank Sinatra arriving to sing with one of Al Capone's cousins at each elbow, had now become personal advisor to Batista for the reforming of gaming and asked him to "clean up" Havana... Gregory H. Hemingway provides us with an anecdote which tells us a lot about the climate that was then reigning in Havana: "Once, when we were driving at a snail's pace through the crowded, narrow backstreets of the city, shots rang out and a man came running towards us with a submachine. He said to our chauffeur, Juan, as he handed him the gun 'Hold this for me, will you please? I have to run.'

'Juan was too surprised to do anything else; but Papa, sitting beside him in the Lincoln convertible, cursed at him under his breath: "You've got your prints all over it now, you bloody fool. Wipe it off and drop it, and let's get the hell out of here.'" As Jorge Valls reminds us, the era of the "dagger planted in the ground" had arrived and everyone had to decide what side they were on. In one of the vignettes in *In Peace as in War*, Guillermo Cabrera Infante tells the story of a man who was beaten to death. Before he died, he remembered the last words of the manifesto he had just written: "Either we shall be free or we shall fall with bullets in our chests." Hemingway could not have ignored all the country people buried alive by the political police, the rebels hung from the branches of the trees, the men who were castrated and left at the side of the road to serve as an example, the hundreds of dead at the sadly infamous "*promenade sanglante*". Between 1952 and 1959, the repression claimed fifty two thousand victims. Those spectacular Cuban sunsets, admired from the window of the hotel Ambos Mundos or from the bridge of the *Anita* or the '*Pilar*', seemed to belong to another world.

One of the saddest moments in Hemingway's life

was surely the day in 1957 that Batista's soldiers killed his dog Black Dog – who, according to Hemingway, had discovered the relationship between "a typewriter and a marrowbone" – during a night raid. This absurd death marked the end of his Cuban dream. Some years later, while he was working on finishing the manuscript of *The Dangerous Summer*, he returned to this tragic episode and confided in A. E. Hotchner: "I knew it was all over for me here the night they killed Black Dog. A Batista search party looking for guns, came barreling in here in the middle of the night and poor Black Dog old and half blind, tried to stand guard at the door of the *Finca*, but a soldier clubbed him to death with the butt of his rifle. Poor old Black Dog. I miss him. In the early morning when I work, he's not hunting lizards beside the pool: and in the evenings when I sit in my chair to read, His chin isn't resting on my foot. I miss Black Dog as much as I miss any friend I ever lost." (*Papa Hemingway*.)

In November 1958, he wrote to his son Patrick that Cuba was really ugly. He added that he was not frightened, but that he was sick of living in a country where no-one was right – and both sides were as atrocious as the other, knowing the kind of things and the murders that would take place when the new ones arrived – and see the abuses of those in power now. He went on to say that they were treated OK, like in all countries, and had very good friends, but that things were bad and the government was appalling. (*Letters*, Ketchum, 24 November 1958.) When Batista fled and Castro entered Havana, Hemingway was not in Cuba, but in Idaho. Of course, someone phoned him to have his reaction on the spot. James R. Mellow observed that it was in two stages. First of all, he replied that he was "delighted", but when the Times correspondent suggested that a revolution always engendered excesses, he asked for his words to be

Habana. Residencias en el Vedado. Vedado Residences.

The Vedado is an area bordered in large part by the Malecón. As this picture shows, at the beginning of the century it was one of the fashionable quarters of Havana. Simone de Beauvoir, who traveled to Cuba, could write " I loved Havana. The Vedado where we were staying has all the attractions of a rich capitalist city: wide avenues and long American cars." (*La Force de L'Age*, Gallimard.).

played down. He was therefore no longer "delighted", but "full of hope". In any case, as in numerous other situations, he could be quoted as saying and doing what he had neither said nor done. Like the press release that confirmed he had bought Batista a drink? Slander, he retorted, adding that he had never met the individual.

In April 1959, Hemingway bought a house with eighteen acres of land at 400, Canyon Run Boulevard, less than two kilometers from Ketchum, near Big Wood river, not far from the Sun Valley winter sports resort. Was he already aware that he would have to leave an island he had loved so much? Without going as far as to say he was pro-Castro, it is clear that his sympathies lay with this man who was not yet the *maximo* leader. He had hailed the departure of Batista with a thundering "*Hijo de puta!*", but he no longer felt strong enough to stay at the *Finca*. His relationship to Castro was not so much ambiguous as nonexistent. Fidel told him that he had taken *For Whom the Bell Tolls* into the mountains with him, like a gue-

rilla's manual... And when he won a fishing competition in 1960 (according to some people, he cheated), it was Hemingway who presented him with the prize. Well... Of course, Hemingway did tell the art critic Kenneth Tynan, at the Floridita, that this revolution was a good revolution, an "honest" revolution. He wasn't the only person to think this at the time. In February 1960, Anastas Mikoïan, the Soviet Trade Minister, who had swiftly taken advantage of the opening left by the United States, seized the opportunity to visit the *Finca Vigía*, where he spent two hours... And what else was there to add to the file that the apothecaries of History never fail to establish, those auctioneers who judge, decree and apportion blame and reward? In November 1959, when he stepped off the plane at the airport of Rancho Boyeros, Hemingway said that this revolution was the "best thing ever to happen to Cuba" and especially, in an aside to Argentinean writer Rodolfo Walsh, that he hoped the Cubans would not consider him a Yankee – "I'm not a Yankee, you know"– but as a Cuban, after which he kissed the Cuban flag and added, in perfect Spanish: "*Vamos a gañar. Nosotros los Cubanos, vamos a gañar.*"

Any solidarity with the struggle led by Castro was purely emotional. The flag he kissed was clearly not the flag of Castroism, but the flag of his fisher friends, of the members of the population he rubbed shoulders with, and who were his company during his stay in Havana. Hemingway never became involved in Cuban politics, and, as he wrote to General Charles T. Lanham, in January 1960, he believed in the "complete necessity of the Cuban revolution." While the political and armed struggles that agitated Havana in the nineteen fifties never mobilized him, nevertheless he was extremely clear-sighted about Castro's rise to power, and as early as January 24, 1956, expressed fears that an excessive reaction on the part of the

In *Our Man in Havana*,
Grahame Greene wrote about
little cream and white houses
belonging to the rich in
Vedado, adding that you
could estimate the wealth
of the owner by the small
number of storeys.

United States would push Cuba into the arms of the Soviets. Given the extent of the US interests in Cuba, Hemingway hoped that the Americans would do everything possible to try to give the Cubans their chance, for the first time. And he prayed that the United States would not stop buying sugar, for it would be the end of everything. It would be like handing Cuba over to the Russians as a gift. As for Castro who, in his speech of June 16, asking the famous question: "What are the rights of revolutionary or non revolutionary writers and artists? Within the revolution, everything; against the revolution, nothing at all." Hemingway, less blinded than Jean-Paul Sartre, had answered fourteen years previously, in a text written after the publication of an essay by Ivan Kachkine, who made of Hemingway a *mens morbida in corpore sano*: Hemingway wrote that he couldn't be a communist because he only believed in one thing: freedom. In the first instance, he wanted to take care of himself and do his work. Then, he wanted to take care of his family. After that he wanted to be able to help his fellow man. But the State, he cared nothing for. As far as he was concerned, the State had always been synonymous with unwarranted taxes. He was in favor of a government reduced to the strict minimum. He felt the writer was like a bohemian, isolated. A good wri-

ter would never like the regime he was living under. His pen would be against it. A writer only had class consciousness if his talent was limited. The Cuban revolution was certainly Latin America's revenge on history, but all the same it should not have instigated a regime that denied the right to freedom. After several return journeys between the United States and his dear *Finca*, Hemingway left Cuba for the last time in July 1960, destination Idaho, with thirty-two cases of luggage. He must surely have noticed the anti-American slogans written on the walls, and the banners with "*Cuba si! Yankee no!*" stretched across the streets.

When Cuba broke off diplomatic relations with the United States in January 1961, Hemingway had already left the island for good. He told A. E. Hotchner: "He [Castro] doesn't bother me personally. I am good publicity for them, so maybe they'd never bother me and let me live on here as always, but I am an American above everything else and I cannot stay here when other Americans are being kicked out and my country is being vilified." A nice example of the integrity of the non-partisan, but thoroughly committed Hemingway. The Havana cycle had turned full circle. Hemingway had succeeded in reaching Cuba, and made his home there for many years. But the Cuba he yearned for and immortalized in his writing had rounded a corner in history; the page was about to be turned; the chapter closed. Hemingway's Cuba, the place he fell in love with and remained faithful to, was no more. The place he had first been introduced to as a kind of paradise was becoming a sort of living hell. And the decline of Havana mirrored the decline of Hemingway himself. The "good times" had come to an end; the "farm with a view," as Martha Gellhorn called it in 1938, closed its doors. Havana entered into the era of the blockade, the innocent intoxication flirting

Enseñada de Atarés.

at each step with disaster. Havana was now unrecognizable, broken, emptied, with no water and no electricity, bloodless, and scarred. The city had lost its sunsets. It had lost its sparkly silver streets. It was trembling on the edge of the shadows. Awaiting tears, awaiting the sleep that she could never find in the marble that now constituted her prison, her roots. However, in this Havana that will never be the same again, dilapidated and solitary, nostalgic, shivered its old southern, reverential past. It was both a full stop and the commencement of a new era. The dollar – that "pain of the dollar", that Zoé Valdès wrote about – was back, admittedly, but disintegration was not yet on the horizon because Havana itself was alive and well. Shaken,

dismembered, it was there in all its rhythm, its saffron diversity, and its Hispanic identity. African and Chinese, Havana was on a human scale but surpassed the population, just as it surpassed the solitude and the horror. Havana was to her residents what Cuba was to the Cubans. The great Cuban poet Lezama Lima, who knew everything about Havana, gives us this last piece of advice: explore Havana in the twilight, never in the stark light of day or at the height of noon: "The light in the morning and the light of dusk, these are the times when the play of lights on Havana are at their best," *against the sunset's towering sea.*

One of the windows of Hemingwayís bedroom. On the right, the antilope killed in Tanganyika in 1933.

NGAJE NGÁI or
The House of the God Beneath the Trees

Ernest Hemingway and Mary Welsh, his fourth wife since March 1946.

A character like me, Hemingway said, has the whole world to chose from, they naturally want to know — why here. Usually don't try to explain. Too complicated. The clear cool mornings when you can work good with just Black Dog awake and the fighting cocks sending out their first bulletins. Where else can you train cocks and fight them and bet those you believe in and be legal. Some people put the arm on fighting cocks as cruel? But what else does a fighting cock like to do. Then there is the bird population —wonder birds, truly — resident and migratory, quail that drink at the swimming pool before the sun comes up.

ERNEST HEMINGWAY
Quoted by A. E. Hotchner in *Papa Hemingway*.

At the end of November 1938, Hemingway made a fourth and last journey to wartime Spain and witnessed the defeat of the republicans on the Ebre. His relationship with Pauline Pfeiffer was in the process of breaking up. His mother, who came down from Key West to try to persuade him against divorce, was given a categorical refusal. The first months of 1939 were an "uneasy" period in Hemingway's life. He spent most of his time shuttling between Key West and Havana and eventually elected residence in the hotel Ambos Mundos. In room 525, which he was familiar with, and that the hotel's director, Manolo Asper, kept permanently available for him, he worked from eight thirty am to three pm on his new manuscript: *For Whom the Bell Tolls*. Martha Gellhorn, the former wife of Bertrand de Jouvenel and a committed journalist, was just back from Europe, and joined him there, planning to continue the writing of her novel *The Stricken Field*. The tropical heat of the summer, and the usual lack of organization at the hotel Ambos Mundos, compelled her to look for a quieter place. About nine miles from Havana, at San Francisco de Paula, an ancient hermitage built in the 18th century by Agustin de Arocha, a Colonel from the Canary

The main entrance of the Finca Vigía which opens into the salon. On the right is Mary Welsh's bedroom window.

The little wooden houses in the village of San Fransisco de Paula where the Finca Vigía is situated.

Isles, she found a rather dilapidated house, that was vast and cool. Built in Spanish colonial style, it had high ceilings, tiled floors, and an enormous living room. It was set in grounds of sixteen acres, and had a swimming pool and tennis courts. Perched on the top of a hill, with a pleasant breeze blowing and an impressive view of the distant lights of Havana, the house was named "*Finca Vigía*" after a watchtower that formerly stood in the vicinity. Set in hilly terrain, near the source of the small rio Luyano, the house was around nine miles from the sea. A detail about the place amused Hemingway: this place was once the theatre for one of the very first commando operations of modern times. As he related in *Defense of the Realm*, in the seventeen sixties, the British had succeeded in infiltrating across the hills to take Havana from behind, while the defenses were too busy riposting to the canon fire from their fleet.

The owner, a certain Roger D'Orn from New Orleans, who owned a cement factory, was asking a hundred dollars a month in rent, which Hemingway

found excessive, but Martha had fallen for the place. She renovated the ruined outhouses with her own personal funds and moved in. Hemingway joined her, but continued to have his mail addressed to calle Obispo – for the sake of appearances. In November 1940, he finally divorced Pauline Pfeiffer. Accusing Hemingway of having deserted the marital home, up till then she had been refusing to legalize their separation. Two weeks later he married Martha Gellhorn and bought the house in December, from the proceeds of the cinema rights from *For Whom the Bell Tolls*, which he had just sold for what was a record amount at the time - $150,000. The sale price of the house was fixed at 18,500 Cuban pesos.

What is the stretch of road like today, that joins San Francisco de Paula and Havana? What remains of the road – *la Carretera Central* was a major highway in the nineteen fifties – that Hemingway traveled so often? In *Islands in the Stream*, he gives a disenchanted and miserable description of it. Hemingway was struck by the pitiful, grotesque shadows that seemed to haunt this much-traveled route: "This was the part he did not like on the road into town. This was really the part he carried the drink for. I drink against poverty, dirt, four-hundred-year-old dust, the nose-snot of children, cracked palm fronds, roofs made from hammered tins, the shuffle of untreated syphilis, sewage in the old beds of brooks, lice on the bare necks of infested poultry, scale on the backs of old men's necks, the smell of old women and the full blast radio, he thought." (*Islands in the Stream.*) When Robert Harling, the correspondent for the London Sunday Times, met Hemingway in December 1954, he noticed that the industrial zone of Havana gave way to a few stalls and workshops open to the winds, with small groups of men, or individual women here and there, Black or Hispanic Cubans sitting on the

The houses of San Fransisco de Paula, along the Carretera Central.

FOLLOWING PAGE: The vegetation around the Finca Vigía is particularly lush: palm trees, orchids, hibiscus, jasmine, avocado and bougainvilleas. This is the realm of Mary Welsh.

steps of their hovels, playing dominos or doing nothing, just staring into space. But what struck him most was the presence, on the road that forked towards Matanzas, of sparkling Chevrolets and Cadillacs, and the occasional run down public service bus succumbing to the race for speed.

From the suburbs of Havana with their indistinct paths winding through the shrubbery of the hills, la Carretera Central and its side-roads hardly seem to have changed at all. The same rows of dilapidated houses, with their little wooden awnings, the same distress, the same sadness, identical filth, corrugated iron, crumbling walls, split roughcast, dirt, dust, disease, mangy dogs, lack of water and food, total destitution, an island adrift in the stream. The *bloqueo* (embargo) decreed by the White House on February 3, 1962, renewed on May 14, 1964 and reinforced ever since by successive Republican or Democratic Presidents, blacklisted hundreds of basic necessities, foodstuffs and medicines, even children's medicines. The *bloqueo* has been in force for thirty-five years.

Meanwhile, back at the *Finca...* Imagine the camera traveling slowly and silently beside the mango trees along the edge of the road leading to the house. The tall palm trees disappear, and the flowers – orchids, hibiscus, jasmine, lovingly chosen by Mary Welsh – Hemingway's fourth wife, a war journalist he married in March 1946 –, the humming birds building their nests in the tropical foliage. The *Finca* is there, with its high walls that resemble ramparts. When Hemingway lived there, the gate was locked, and the perimeter wall boasted five rows of barbed wire. There was a signpost supposedly to deter unwanted visitors: "No visitors except appointment." On a second, smaller sign, a second message was scribbled: "*Se prohibe entrar terminantemente sin frevia audencia por telf...*" Only those people who have made an appointment are authorized to enter here. This makes me think of Hemingway's white beard. It didn't give him the air of respectability of a patriarch. It was only an external sign of his age, another mask, and a necessary protection, like the gate. When you look at it, suddenly, everything becomes clear. In an article published in February 1955, Alejo Carpentier relates a strange experience he had at the *Finca*. 'Monument en Arbeit', the painting by Paul Klee, was hanging on the wall next to an open window that looked onto the luxuriant garden, full of palm trees and bougainvilleas. While he was looking at it, this painting took on a new dimension: "In an environment like this, Paul Klee's work burst into color, became tropicalized, blended utterly harmoniously with a landscape that, at first sight, it had nothing in common with" (*Chroniques*, Gallimard.) Hemingway, in his *Finca*, is like these paintings. Impregnated with foreign elements, he became other, took on a universal force. In this context, he became more solid and grander. A lesser being would not have resisted such exuberant vegetation. Imposing, he stands his ground firmly and endures. This is the lesson to be learnt from the gate. A procession marching in the direction of his life's work. Ideally, we should reread Hemingway with Cuba in mind, with the physical and emotional presence of Cuba. Reread *A Moveable Feast* and think of Cuba. Try to discern Cuba in *The Garden of Eden*. Find traces of Havana in the *By Line Chronicles*. Feel the ancestral force of the Gulf Stream in the urban pages of *Islands in the Stream*. Then push open the gate.

The first impression is of being surrounded in lush vegetation. Mary professed that the major difficulty in gardening in Cuba was to maintain a balance of color. The rich shades of green, the bright splashes of hibiscus and bougainvilleas, cheese plants, avocado trees with fruit almost as bright and shiny as their leaves,

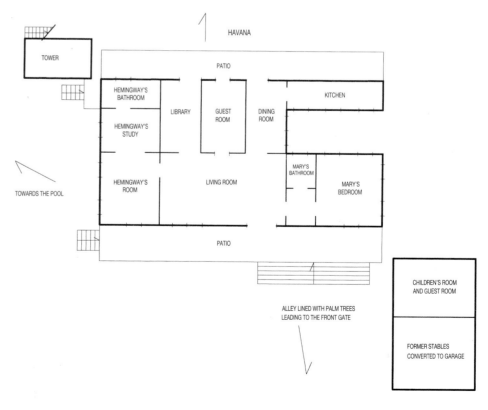

PREVIOUS PAGE: The swimming pool where Ava Gardner bathed nude. Quails came here at dawn to quench their thirst. Hemingway swam there daily.

OPPOSITE: The drawing room. Mary Welsh as reponsible for the layout of the room. It was she who designed the furniture with the help of Otto Bruce. On the right, the armchair in which Hemingway liked to read. Within arms reach, the drinks table he made himself. At the far end , the record collection and a trophy similar to those in many other rooms – a stag shot in 1930 in Wyoming.

the royal palm trees a myriad of grays in the first light of day, flowerless flamboyant trees, flowers with green shimmers, the luxuriant pungency of a whole jungle, with creepers and sighing breezes, interlapping horizons and all around, the chalky summits of the hills, brown in winter, green in summer, and in front, the majestic ceiba that is no longer there.

This tree has a story to tell. Its mossy trunk, with smooth bark the color of an elephant's skin, was covered in orchids; its enormous roots cracked the walls of the house, and pushed up the paving stones on the patio. One day, Mary committed a sacrilege that made Hemingway furious. Taking advantage of his absence, she had one of the roots cut, because it was pushing up the paving stones on the patio. Hemingway had forbidden anyone to touch the roots. He loved that tree, of course, but his decision was not a whim, for the ceiba is in fact a sacred tree in voodoo rites. Amidst the fifteen acres of flowers and vegetables, pastures and fruits trees on Hemingway's property, it represented la *santería*, the practical, non-metaphysical religion that bears witness to the presence of African religions on the island. Like Black Cubans, Hemingway had always preferred sorcery to conventional medicine, and feared evil spells. He was aware that life had magical aspects and was familiar with the fascinating action of spells and counter spells. The little fiber and wood dolls at the *Finca*, African fetishes pierced with needles, show Hemingway's interest in black magic. Each day, he communed with his own witch doctor, writing, which, just like the sorcerer in la *santería*, throws shells in the air to predict the future and read lucky or unlucky numbers on the wings of a moth.

Between the mangos (there were eighteen different species in the grounds of Hemingway's property) and the palms, a sloping path. A vast center divider strip. And there was the house, with its high white ramparts.

The magazine rack in the living room carried periodicals and newspapers from all over the world.

Hemingway's two sons, Gregory and Patrick, in the drawing-room.

Wyoming deer that he killed in 1930. There were animal skins strewn on the floor. The furniture was old, comfortable, almost banal: several tables, a large sofa, a few armchairs – including his favorite one – covered in Liberty print, with now faded red and white motifs, and some pieces of furniture designed by Mary Welsh and made by Francisco Curto. There is an old Capehart gramophone, and a collection of records showing Hemingway's somewhat ecclectic tastes: Gerome Kern and Brahms, the hymns of the international brigades, Navajo Indian music, Manuel de Falla and Beguines from Martinique, Carmen Cavallero, Beny Goodman, Verdi, Mozart, Schubert, Art Tatum, Morton Gould, Hungarian gypsy music, Flamenco, Russian Folk Songs, Oklahoma Songs and other Mexican Cancionero... nine hundred different titles, including a recording of the American Constitution. Between the living room and the dining room there was a magazine stand, which used to be filled with periodicals and newspapers from the United States and from all over the world: Collierís, Sports Afield, The Reporter, Life, Spectator, Time, Farm and Country, The New Statesman, The Tatler, The Field, etc.

As in most of the rooms, especially Hemingway's room, there was a huge bookcase. The one in the living room was the largest of all. It contained volumes

There were steps leading up to it. In Cuba, the heat can be stifling, and the Finca had neither fans nor air conditioning, except in Hemingway's room. He never switched it on, though, because the noise disturbed him.

A massive table dominated the immense dining room, where convivial dinners were held. This was the room where the famous Miró painting, The Farm, was displayed. It was one of the major pieces in Hemingway's modest gallery. Off the dining room was the equally vast living room, twenty yards long. The walls were decorated with stuffed trophies of some of the animals Hemingway had killed in Africa, deer with majestic antlers, strange, static objects that tell us about Hemingway the hunter, like the head of the brown

The drinks table Hemingway designed so that he could easily reach the bottles without leaving his armchair, on the right of the photograph. In 1940, Hemingway told brother Leicester about an evening's drinking, where he started out with absinthe, then drank a bottle of red wine at dinner, then switched to vodka in the town before the pelota match. He then finished on whiskies and soda till three in the morning.

of contemporary literature, natural history, treatises on military history, collections of poems and plays, essays and novels, cookery books, history books, geography books. Three hundred books in French and nine hundred in Spanish. Here and there was a book by Hemingway. The bookcases at the *Finca* held almost five thousand volumes. The impression that this strange sanctuary evoked was not one of untidiness, but of overabundance. Today, everything in the house is tidy and orderly, but all observers agree that when Hemingway lived there, every last square foot available was invaded, brimming over, appropriated by the vast array of items that constitute the testimonials to a life. During a visit to the *Finca*, George Plimpton was surprised to find, all on the same book-shelves, *The Common Reader* by Virginia Woolf, *The Republic* by Charles A. Beard, *Shakespeare and The Dyer's Hand* by Alden Brooks, poems by T. S. Eliot and a book on hunting in Africa, an essay on the Battle of Little Big Horn and *How Young to Look*, by a certain Peggy Wood! The attentive reader could also pick out from this personal library original editions dedicated by the following authors: James Joyce, Scott Fitzgerald, Gertrude Stein, Sherwood Anderson, John Dos Passos, Ford Madox Ford, Ezra Pound, etc. And, continuing along the shelves, would come across the biographies of Eleanor Roosevelt, Custer, Van Gogh, Garibaldi, Buffalo Bill, essays on baseball, *Gil Blas* by Santillane, *The Roots of Heaven* by Romain Gary, *Test Pilot* by Neville Duke, *The Fisherman's Handbook,*

The dining room. Ernest Hemingway and Mary Welsh liked to entertain their friends. *The Farm*, painted by Miró, hung in this room for twenty two years. On each side of the opening to the drawing room hang a pair of long-horns killed during hunting trips in Idaho.

the puzzle, which mustn't be forgotten, was a piece of pure copper he used as a paperweight when the easterly wind was blowing. There were no chairs. French windows led onto the patio; on another bookcase there was a silver frame containing a photograph of his two sons, Patrick and Gregory. A short text published in Paris Review, in 1958, describes the writer at work: "Early in the morning he gets up and, standing in front of his desk, he concentrates totally. He only moves to shift his weight from one foot to the other, sweats profusely when his work is going well, is agitated like a child, irritated or unhappy when the grace of the art momentarily escapes him and he remains a slave to his self-imposed discipline until around noon."

There is little point enumerating the rooms at the *Finca* one by one. Suffice it to say that the kitchen, which is closed to visitors, as is the *sótano* (the cellar) – is to the north, in one of the two wings of the house – the other is Mary's room –, and that, when the wind gets up, the branches of the flamboyant tree beat noisily against the walls and the windows. Another interesting detail is that the bathroom, vast and cluttered with an impressive medical arsenal, has an unusual feature. Ernest Hemingway used to watch his weight carefully and check his heart rate, and so – with the

Balzac, Benito Perez Galdos, *Verdun* by Jules Romains, *Journal d'un salaud* by Henri Queffélec, Paul Morand, Gide, Simenon, and so on.

The living room gave directly onto the yellow-tiled bedroom where Ernest Hemingway used to start work early in the morning. A bed, more bookshelves, a massive, dark chest supporting a leopard skin, a large table covered in stacks of letters, press cuttings, souvenirs, reminders, fetishes. In the continuation, a study, with a large worktable he never used, since he wrote standing up. On top of the bookcase to the right of his bed he had placed his Royal portable typewriter, and a wooden writing case he used to write the characters dialogues for his books in pencil. The last element in

The cutlery stamped with the emblems of the Finca: The three mountains of Paris (Montparnasse, Montmartre, and St Genevieve) and the three hills of San Fransisco de Paula; the arrowheads of the Ojibway Indians of Michigan, and the Captainís insignia worn by Mary and Hemingway during the war.

OPPOSITE LEFT: Friends reunited. Sometimes these reunions would turn into a brawl. Hemingway once threw a salad at the back of an official of the American Embassy. He then threw his steak across the table.

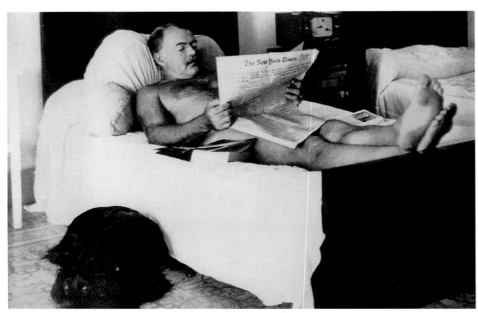

At the bottom of the bed, Black Dog, Hemingway's favourite dog, killed by soldiers come to carry out a search in the Finca.

OPPOSITE: "For a good part of his adult life Hemingway was, of course, a ten-goal drinker, and he could hold it well. He was far more disciplined in this regard, though, than the legend may suggest. Frequently when he was working hard, he would drink nothing, except perhaps a glass or two of wine with meals." Roy Mannige, Atlantic Monthly, August 1965.

RIGHT HAND PAGE: Hemingway's bed covered in books and letters. He never slept there.

on bull fighting, packets of letters held together by elastic bands, all kinds of documents and papers; a map of "Nyasaland Portuguese East Africa," knives lined up on a red matador's cape, FFI armbands, a bat, a frog and a lizard in jars filled with formalin, monumental pencil sharpeners, etc. Of course, this untidiness, like the library that Captain Nemo gathers in his Nautilus, has been stopped in time. Looking at the *Finca*, we could also exclaim that "the world ended for me the day my Nautilus plunged for the first time beneath the waves. And since the, I would like to believe that humanity has neither thought nor written." However, the arrested world of the *Finca* throws a strange light on the man who spent twenty years of

same carpenter's pencil that he used to write the characters' dialogues in his novels — he noted the dates he took his blood pressure, his weight, the numbers of his prescriptions and a fair amount of other information of a medical and pharmaceutical nature, on the left-hand wall, behind the door.

To come back to the curious impression of bric-a-brac that reigned in the *Finca*, methods of filing, tidying, orderliness or disorderliness can reveal a lot about a person, lay them bare. Now, what do we see? In Hemingway's bedroom, a weird assortment of traces of his past lined up in single file: a small sachet containing the teeth of carnivores, two broken alarm clocks, shoe horns, a pen with no ink on an onyx stand, wooden sculptures of a zebra, a wild boar, a rhinoceros and a lion. And on top of one of the bookcases in the living-room: a giraffe made of wooden beads, a small jade tortoise, a Venetian gondola, a furry monkey, a model US Navy biplane, small-scale models of locomotives, two Jeeps and a mechanical bear. And everywhere, old newspapers, publications

his life there. Hemingway's remark to George Plimpton, the journalist who asked him what he thought of this strange accumulation of souvenirs, is fascinating: "In the opinion of their owner," wrote George Plimpton, "these relics have as much importance as the three pairs of buffalo horns decorating one of the walls of the room. They are less precious due to their impressive size, no doubt, than for the risks he took and the heroic feats perpetrated to acquire them. While he willingly acknowledged the slightly obsessive nature of these collections, Hemingway was not very willing to give more away, as if he could feel that silence was the best way to protect the secret that made each of these objects so valuable to him." (George Plimpton, The Paris Review, spring 1958.)

Remember the death of Harry, in *The Snows of Kilimanjaro*. He had not been able to solve the enigma of the leopard found at an altitude of eighteen thousand feet, near the western summit of the mountain that the Masai called "Ngaje Ngái," the house of the god. With death approaching, he tried to recover the truth of lost impressions. He tried to cling to fragments, to the fleeting images that once fed his writer's inspiration. He tried to remember the name of the hotel he stayed in while he was in Paris, at all costs. But he was not looking for sentimental nostalgia, he didn't want a memory, he wanted the word itself, the name as such. Just like Hemingway who surrounded himself not with souvenirs, but with the objects themselves. Not the souvenir of the wooden African statues acquired in Machakos, but the actual statues themselves; and two prong-horn heads, and the lizard that was wounded in the *Finca*, and the Stetson bought in Nairobi, and the two lion skulls brought back from his first safari in 1933-1934, and the key to a cabin in the *Normandie* steamer, the ammunition taken from the German soldiers during the Second World War, and

Hemingway in front of his typewriter. He wrote standing up. Rising at dawn, he finished work around 1 p.m.

Writing for Hemingway was neither quick nor easy, but always a question of blood and tears. He worked on a Royal and wrote the character dialogues by hand. Ava Gardner asked him one day if he had ever consulted a psychiatrist. "This is my psychiatrist", he said, pointing to his typewriter.

the koudou that was so worn out it was removed in 1986. The writer, to be able to write, had to surround himself with sensations, and only the truth, encapsulated in these objects, could prevent those sensations from fading.

One misty day in Cuba, when Hemingway was feeling low, he said that if he could start all over again, he would like to paint. Even though several paintings have been removed, a glance around the *Finca* shows that Hemingway was an enlightened collector. He acquired a small number of paintings, each chosen with a discerning eye, and each with its own particular story: Miró, Juan Gris, Klee, Braque, André Masson, Waldo Pierce. A watercolor depicting Kilimanjaro; a Flemish still life; Suerte de Baras, a painting by Roberto Domingo; copies of Don Manuel Osorio, Manrique de Zuñiga, Goya; wild ducks by Roger Preuss; a painting by Paul R. Hynckes; and not forgetting hunting sketches by Daumier – "What a stroke of luck! I've killed a sparrow! I won't have to go back empty-handed!" – or the copies of the *Monumenti della Civilta pittorica italiano*, from the celebrated Collezione Silvana... Hemingway found *The Farm*, by Miró, in a café in Montparnasse. The poet Evan Shipman also wanted to buy it. They played dice over it. Hemingway won but, as he didn't have any money, he had to have a whip round and borrow the 5,000 francs he needed to pay for it. He acquired the *Guitar Player*, by Juan Gris, in Paris in 1931. Back from Spain, he was finishing *Death in the Afternoon* and thought about using it as the frontispiece for his novel, but in the end he chose another painting by Juan Gris, which he also owned: *The Bullfighter*. As for the portrait of Hemingway by Waldo Pierce, a friend of John Reed's and a veteran from the First World War, it was done on April 1st, 1929, at Key West.

It was Gertrude Stein who introduced Hemingway to painting and the painters of his generation. In her salon, he met Picasso, Masson and Matisse. Painting played a major role in his life. He could sit for hours, he said, just looking at a Titian. In Paris, he paid long visits to the Jeu de Paume Museum to admire the masterpieces of impressionism, and he also frequented the Musée du Luxembourg: In the New Yorker, in 1957, Hemingway wrote that when his stomach was empty and the museum free, he went to the museum. He went on to say he learnt to write while looking at the paintings. In 1953, when he went back to Spain, he went immediately to the Prado and in the letter he sent to Bernard Berenson (*Selected Letters*), he wrote:

"I wish to hell I could paint." A. E. Hotchner tells an amusing story. When he was visiting the Prado with Hemingway, as they were leaving the room where the Goyas were exhibited, Hemingway led him to a small room to show him the woman he had loved the most faithfully in his life... She was the *Portrait of a Woman* by Andrea del Sarto!

In a chapter in the Nick Adams stories, "On writing", Nick, who wanted to write the way Cézanne painted, confided that he wanted to write on the countryside in such a way that it would have the same presence as Cézanne's in his pictures. To do this, he went on, you had to pull it out from inside yourself. In an interview with a journalist in 1958, in answer to the question "who are your masters in literature?," Hemingway added a series of painters: le Tintoret, Jérôme Bosch, Bruegel, Patenier, Goya, Giotto, Cézanne, Van Gogh, Gauguin. He added: "I mentioned a certain number of painters, since painting has taught me as much about my work as writers." (The Paris Review, spring 1958.)

Hemingway knew how to listen, read and observe. He loved painting, was familiar with it and did not hesitate to write about it. In 1934, he devoted an essay to Joan Miró in *Les Cahiers d'Art*; in February 1935, he defended Spanish painter Luis Quintanilla in the columns of Esquire and published several articles on Cuban painter Antonio Gattorno. This appreciation of the visual arts led Hemingway to the conclusion that artists and writers were confronted with the same problem: how to represent reality. *In Death in the Afternoon*, there are passages devoted to Velazquez, Goya and Miró. In *Across the River and Into the Trees*, the wounded hero, Richard Cantwell, was a keen art lover. In *Islands in the Stream*, Thomas Hudson, novelist and artist, in a famous dialogue with his cat Boise, gives the cat advice in way that makes us feel it was

In Hemingway's bedroom, the picture of his two sons Patrick and Gregory. In the foreground, mounted on a medallion, a picture of Ernest Hemingway and his second wife, Pauline Pfeiffer, taken in the 1920's.

Hemingway himself speaking: "You'd be better off if you liked pictures. […] That was the great thing about pictures; you could love them with no hopelessness at all. You could love them without sorrow and the good ones made you happy because they had done what you had always tried to do. So it was done and it was all right, even if you failed to do it."

To have more peace and quiet in the house, Hemingway had an extension built next to the garage, down below the driveway. The extension had three bedrooms, for accommodating visiting friends and children. It wasn't enough, however, and Mary had a white tower built in 1947, in order to provide Ernest Hemingway with a more suitable place to work than proofs there. He soon gave up the tower and went back to his room in the *Finca* where he could hear the familiar sounds of the house. The tower was too solitary for him, and he abandoned it to the cats. The whole gang slept, ate and reproduced there. They all lived there, with the exception of a few privileged members of the cat population, Crazy Christian, Friendless' Brother and Ecstasy, who were given the honor of freedom of the house!

Hemingway had always loved animals, from grizzly bears to fighting cocks, including dogs, owls and lizards, which he occasionally healed, but his favorite animals of all were cats. There were up to fifty-seven cats at the *Finca Vigía*! He even said he had produced a new breed by crossing angoras with Cuban cats, and he gave each one a more extravagant name than the last, all of which contained the "s" sound: Boise, Missouri, Spendi, Ambrosy who lived at the *Finca* for sixteen years and died in 1969, etc. Then there were Tester, Dilinger, Boissy d'Anglas, Willy, F. Puss, and Mooky. When other cats at the *Finca Vigía*, killed Crazy Christian, one of his favorite cats, in 1946, he wrote a poem for him:

> *To Crazy Christian*
> *There was a cat named Crazy Christian*
> *Who never lived long enough to screw*
> *He was gay hearted, young and handsome*
> *And all the secrets of life he knew*
> *He would always arrive on time for breakfast*
> *Scamper on your feet and chase the ball*
> *He was faster than any polo pony*
> *He never worried a minute at all*
> *His tail was a plume that scampered with him*
> *He was black as night and fast as light.*
> *So the bad cats killed him in the fall.*
> *(88 poems)*

In the first chapter in the second book of *Islands in*

Ladies on the Banks of the River, 1927. Canvas by Antonio Gattorno (1904–1980), the Cuban artist to whom Hemingway devoted several articles.

the impromptu study in his room which was always cluttered. There were three stories: on the first storey, the bathroom. The second was intended to house the cats. On the top floor was the hide-away study, furnished with a huge bookcase full of military works, comfortable armchairs, a worktable; and windows opening onto palm trees and the green hills rolling down to the sea. But nothing went according to plan, for Ernest Hemingway never used this study, except on rare occasions. From time to time he would correct some

Air conditioning unit installed in Hemingway's room by Mary Welsh. He never used it as he found it too noisy.

In an article published in the Paris Review in spring 1958, Hemingway wrote that "after six hours writing, I feel as exhausted and as satisfied as if I had spent all that time in bed with my darling wife."

RIGHT: Hemingway's study. On the wall, the buffalo killed on a hunt in Tanganyika in 1934. The table is covered in an assortment of items: a drawing by Renata Borgitti, photographs of Mary Welsh, German military badges brought back from France, some statuettes bought during a trip to east Africa, a magazine article referring to Zelda and Scott Fitzgerald, some knives and a feather from an American vulture.

FOLLOWING PAGE: Desk in the study. Cartridges from a Winchester 20 and from a Western, Remmington Umc. Super-X, 6.5 calliber. George Plimpton, who visited Hemingway in 1958, wrote in the Paris Review (spring 1958) of the "apparent confusion and disarray of a man enamoured with harmony but incapable of letting go of the smallest knick-knack, especially if there was any sentimental value attached to it."

the Stream, called "Cuba", there is a long dialogue covering several pages, full of humor and tenderness, between Boise, a kitten found at Cojímar, and Thomas Hudson. Exasperated by the presence of all these cats, one day Martha decided to have some of them castrated. She said she wanted to stop them from so much inbreeding that was producing malformed and blind kittens. Hemingway was both furious and hurt, and never forgave her. Years later, Jeffrey Meyers reported that he had said, of his favorite cat that it was strange that he really hated women, and that it was a woman who sent him to have his balls cut off. (*Hemingway*.)

Before it was taken over by the cats, the Tower was supposed to be the place for writing. The major business of Hemingway, and of every self-respecting wri-

ter. A painful, indispensable business, which, according to Paul Auster, doesn't cure anyone of anything. According to Hemingway, the work of writing required the same devotion as the work of a priest. Yes, writing is a down-to-earth, physical business. When Hemingway was in the process of writing a book, he was completely absorbed by the task. At the end of the day, he carefully noted in a notebook or on a blackboard the number of words he had written. Writing is a physical activity. Hemingway wrote slowly, with difficulty. For days, weeks, even months on end, he would rise at dawn, re-read the pages he had written the previous day, make a few corrections here and there, then continue from where he had left off. From that last sentence or last word, the machinery ground back into action. Hemingway immersed himself in his work and projected himself into his work. The packet of sheets of paper was there, at dawn, at that peaceful hour when there is no-one to disturb you and it is cool, or even cold, and you start to work and heat yourself up by working. In a letter to Harvey Breit, he couldn't have been more direct: The crucial problem in Cuba, he said, in essence, was to be in condition very early in the morning and to finish your daily work before noon, for after that "the sweat pours from your armpits and makes the manuscript unusable". Writing is always dangerous, never finished. He rewrote the conclusion to *A Farewell to Arms* thirty-two times and revised the proofs around thirty times. In an interview for the New Yorker, in January 1947, he was quoted as saying that if anyone tried to improve their work, starting over and over again, then it was he "for I sometimes throw forty or fifty versions of the first chapter into the wastepaper basket!". He added that writing was the work of Sisyphus. His manuscripts, most of which are kept in the Kennedy library in Boston, show the meticulous care he took over them, which sometimes bordered on the obsessional, with seemingly endless corrections, scoring out, censoring and cutting.

The vocabulary he used to talk about his labors as a writer is most instructive: "I'm in the middle of a ford", or: "I would like to strip the language to purify it, strip it bare to the bone." (Saint Louis Star-Times, May 1941.) To Ava Gardner who one day asked him incredulously if he had never consulted a psychiatrist, he said, pointing to his portable Corona typewriter: "There is my psychiatrist." And when the day's work was finally over, you had to wait till the next day before you could re-immerse yourself in this grave business called writing, and then nothing could affect

you, nothing could happen to you, nothing meant anything to you until the next day when you could start again. It was the waiting for the next day that Hemingway found difficult to bear. Writing is a way of postponing death, a way of beating loneliness. On October 24, 1954, the jury of the Swedish Academy awarded Ernest Hemingway the Nobel Prize for literature. He did not attend the ceremony; the reason invoked being the painful after-effects of the accidents he had been involved in during his Africa safari. The United States Ambassador to Sweden, John M. Cabot, was asked to read his speech for him. Hemingway's speech included the following passage: "Writing, at its best, is a lonely life. Organizations for writers palliate the writer's loneliness but I doubt if they improve his writing. He grows in public stature as he sheds his loneliness and often his work deteriorates. For he does his work alone and if he is a good enough writer he must face eternity, or the lack of it, each day. For a true writer each book should be a new beginning where he tries again for something that is beyond attainment.

At the entrance to the bathroom, placed on the red cape of a American bullfighter Sydney Franklin, knives from different countries and eras: short sword of Alalem warrior, 19th century Arab dagger, etc.

In the Crystal inkwell, the keys to the Ritz and the Normandie.

The stetson he bought in Nairobi, in 1953, and Hemingway's hunting vest.

Hemingway with his cats. He had fifty-seven in all!

He should always try for something that has never been done or that others have tried and failed. Then sometimes, with great luck, he will succeed. How simple the writing of literature would be if it were only necessary to write in another way what has already been written. It is because we have had such great writers in the past that a writer is driven far out past where he can go, out to where no one can help him. I have spoken too long for a writer. A writer should write what he has to say and not speak it. Again I thank you."

What more could we say? Hemingway criticized Scott Fitzgerald for writing too "solemnly". For Hemingway, it was understood that the important thing was to write as well as possible, to learn and live at the same time, and to finish what you had started. In this way, he did not so much deliver a "testimony" of our times, but gave us a scoop on his own personal reaction: he did not write as well as he could or as he wanted to, but as he was obliged to. He listened to the monster within, and invited us to share his intuitions,

his feeling for life. "Sweating blood and tears", he let the pages pile up and invade his life – "whether consciously or not, there's always a novel going on in my head" –, he made writing his main vice and his greatest pleasure. "Writing is a tough trade. Don't get mixed up in it if you can help it" he would advise those who wrote to him for advice. His son, Gregory H., won a writing competition by copying a short story by Turgenev and simply changing the setting and the names. "So many things make us smile or laugh," wrote Hemingway. "In the United States, they thought bull racing was a joke. Ezra Pound thought fishing was a joke. Lots of people think poetry is a joke." But writing is no joke.

Where did Hemingway's writing come from? From formative books, influences, meetings, models, critics, contradictions. Among the Russian writers who influenced Hemingway were Tolstoy and Turgenev; in the Anglo-Saxon field, Mark Twain, Henry James, Yeats, Henry Fielding, Emerson, Thoreau; but also Stendhal, Flaubert, Maupassant, Thomas Mann. Among contemporary influences, his acquaintance with Gertrude Stein was decisive, as were his relationships with Ford Madox Ford, Ezra Pound, Joyce and Sherwood Anderson. But there was another influence on which Hemingway drew with delight and efficacy: journalism. Gertrude Stein, who said that she had

Hemingway owned numerous
pairs of shoes, and was
usually seen in mocassins
with no socks.

never met any geniuses other than God, Picasso and herself, was wrong when she advised the young Hemingway to give up journalism if he really wanted to become a writer. Ernest Hemingway is one of the few major American authors who did not study at a higher education establishment. And so the seven months he spent working on the Kansas City Star, from April 1917, were of decisive importance for him. Leo Lania was not mistaken: this period helped to "shape and determine his style, his art, his whole life". (*Hemingway*.) He became a man of Letters at a very young age, and the time he spent as a journalist convinced him that narrative language could be colloquial, and be drawn from the language of popular

American expression, and that the writer should not hesitate to make use of the most explicit slang. His rigorous writing can therefore be situated at the confluence of two major trends in American literature: naturalism and symbolism. Hemingway freed American prose from emphasis and pathos, and created a modern realism achieved through brief, incisive dialogues, a literature whose first task was the insatiable search for *le mot juste*.

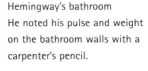
Hemingway's bathroom
He noted his pulse and weight on the bathroom walls with a carpenter's pencil.

His rejection of pretension, masks and special effects was something he learnt the necessity of from journalism. Admittedly, art is not "loyal"; it makes a virtue of the lie and doesn't hesitate to bend the truth in order to make it the more evident, but this was not the reason behind Hemingway's meticulousness. In the article he sent to Esquire Magazine in December 1934, Hemingway, who was only thirty-five years old at the time, gives us a precious lesson in literature, when he tells us that the most difficult thing in the world is to write perfectly sincere prose about human beings, because, first of all, you have to know your subject, and then you have to know how to write. Writing is a serious business, the writer should only write about what he knows, and always be sincere. There are a large number of quotes from Hemingway on the subject of this primordial sincerity, in various

Hemingway found this injured lizzard at the *Finca*, and tried to save it. After it died he preserved it in a jar of formalin and placed it on one of the shelves in the bathroom.

The library was originally a guest room. As the books accumulated, Mary Welsh transformed it in 1949. She designed the furniture with Francisco Castro.

In the library: Note the Bullfight poster, and at the foot of the stepladder, on the right, the famous *Collezione Silvana*, a collection of monograms on the great Italian painters, Mantegna, Fra Angelico, etc.

newspapers and periodicals of the time – "The writer's first obligation is sincerity, being original, for a writer, is being oneself," "Seeing, feeling, expressing – everything is there! In other words, go down into yourself, ask yourself questions, find the vital force that enables you to talk with sincerity about things you know about, and that you care about". Sincerity, however, is not synonymous with truth. The writer is sincere when talking from the depths of his being, and the order that reigns there may well be secretly disorderly, chaotic, emotional, even if well-arranged. In this American work in which six languages are spoken – in addition to English - Spanish, Italian, French, Swahili and German –, the author is playing a role as imposter that consists in beginning with language and

ending up with fiction. And he applies to the letter the wish expressed by Kipling: "first get your facts, then do with them what you will", adding a dimension that is purely his own: enumerating reality. By taking an inventory of beings and things, Hemingway first of all seizes his own reality, sets off in search of his own identity, and tries to give us an irrefutable definition of experience. For Hemingway: All good books are alike in that they are truer than if they really happened and after you are finished reading one you will feel that it all happened to you and afterwards it all belongs to you: the good and the bad, the ecstasy, the remorse and sorrow, the people and the places and how the weather was. If you can get so that you can give that to people, then you are a writer. In this kind of literature that never uses a word too many and seeks salvation through perfection, Hemingway compared the integrity of the writer to the virginity of a young girl. Once it has been lost, it can never be recovered. To write is to multiply your points of view about life, and in so doing the writer can learn a lot about himself and about writing. In this way, the writer can transmit to the reader, through the writing, the *frisson sacré* or sacred emotion that moves the writer. In this way, the writer can communicate the impression felt and the emotion which is nothing other than the result, the infinitesimal traces left by the contact between oneself and the outside world: emotions are the only facts that it is worthwhile living and remembering in order to create literature.

So many questions have been raised. One of the major ones is how do you become a great writer when you love the world, love living in it, and enjoy the company of people in general, and certain people in particular? In an article published in the New York Herald Tribune Book Review, on December 29, 1946, Hemingway admitted that if he had not imposed a rigorous schedule on himself, he would never have been able to write another line. He added that his biggest failing was his sociability, and that a writer was not like a business magnate with a whole bureaucratic organization to protect him from his friends. At the *Finca*, friends dropped by, the Nobel Prize attracted bores. In the nineteen twenties, when Hemingway lived in rue Notre-Dame-des-Champs, in Paris, his friend the poet Archibald MacLeish wrote a poem in which he wondered what would happen to "this boy as lithe as a sleepy panther, when fame would hit him"? Hemingway repeatedly told the people who came to interview him that they should not raise their hopes, for he would not give anything vital away in his interviews because the essence of his thought was to be

Stamp bearing the amusing and now famous inscription "I never write letters".

In the library, the leopard killed by Hemingway on his second safari in 1953-1954.

found in his books. To no avail; the throng around the swimming pool at the *Finca* forced him to divide visitors up into two groups: dear friends, who were invited and on whom attention was lavished, and intruders that the barbed wire on the gate, the growling of Black Dog and the dissuasive sign written in Hispanic-American combined did not effectively deter.

Around that swimming pool, where the water became cooler the deeper you went, in the shade of the majestic trees swaying in the gentle breeze that would subside completely at nightfall, while the reflection of the bamboos and poplars danced merrily on the surface of the water, friendship could give free reign to its ephemeral and tender vapors like those of the smoke of a good tobacco. Mary tended the temple and tried to give a semblance of order to these round the clock parties where the whisky flowed freely, vying with mature Cuban rum. The lights never went out as stars of the cinema, Flamenco dancers, bull fighters, all these celebrities, some with impeccable credentials, others with dubious reputations, lived out their little dramas, exposed their plans and ambitions, expressed their remorse, making music or mayhem in this marvelous, carefree existence. How could she hope to protect Hemingway from this star-studded burlesque cast of Bengal lights? Mary said that she tried to keep the

peace from Monday till Thursday, but weekends were always eventful, even riotous.

Friendship was not a recent discovery for Hemingway. At the *Finca*, he was only pursuing what for him had long been a necessity. Back in the days when he lived in Paris, he was already constantly surrounded by friends; in Spain, with a war going on all around, had turned his room at the Gaylord hotel into a base where friends, journalists and visitors could drop in for a drink or a bite to eat. There was good music on the turntable and the noise of typewriters mingled with the melodies. Friendship is a way of life and a philosophy. Among the regular guests at the *Finca* featured a good number of Cuban and Spanish friends. Roberto

The library. The photograph shows Ernest Hemingway and Mary Welsh, on the patio, in the shade of the arbour.

Herrera, the former Republican Doctor who sought refuge in Cuba after the Spanish Civil War, Sinsky Dunabeita, the Basque fisherman, a hardened drinker and a hard nut to crack, Father Don Andrés, known as the Black Priest, who had been expelled from Spain after the end of the war for having exhorted his parishioners to take up arms. These Spanish veterans could sometimes be heard striking up Civil War chants and singing in unison, in the wrong key, the hymn of the Fifth Regiment! Alongside the Spanish contingent there were also, of course, friends from Cuba: Mario Menocal (Mayito), who had fought Machado, a boxer and hunter particularly fond of gin and champagne; Elicio Arguelles, owner of the Habana-Madrid Fronton; Thorwald Sanchez, cigar smoker and inventor of the daiquiri lollypop; George Brown, a former boxer who trained Hemingway... And there were others, including a great number of Basque pelot players.

Some faithful friends who did not live in Cuba would also come to visit the residents at the *Finca*. Among them were Gary Cooper, with whom Hemingway talked of nothing other than the weather, hunting and Hollywood. Then there was Ingrid Bergman. Gregory H., Hemingway's son, told of a memorable evening during which, as a child, he watched his father and his friends make fools of themselves in her presence: "Some women are noted for producing a state of temporary insanity in their admirers, but with Miss Bergman the insanity was permanent. – She'd say something inane like 'I always carry

Ingrid Bergman came to the Finca Vigía several times. She played opposite Gary Cooper in Sam Wood's cinema adaptation of *For Whom the bell Tolls*. She was Maria to Gary Cooper's Robert Jordan.

Mask of the Makondé tribe brought back from Hemingway's second African safari in 1953-1954. Also in the library.

an extra pair of stockings in my bag, because you're always getting runs in them and where can you find a pair in the middle of an evening?'. And Papa, whose only possible interest in her lingerie was how to get it off her, would say, 'Yes, Ingrid, that's a very practical thing to do, very practical. It shows you have real common sense, daughter.'" (*Hemingway: Papa.*) Ava Gardner was also part of Hemingway's *entourage* in Cuba, and legend has it that she bathed nude in the swimming pool at the *Finca*. The only person among Hemingway's close friends who never came to the Finca, even though he begged her to come, was Marlene Dietrich. Hemingway had known her since 1934, and he had affectionately nicknamed her "the Kraut". He loved to listen to her records, and wrote her letters described as "amusing, sad, compassionate and sometimes irresistible".

Then there was a sort of third category of passing friends, sometimes turned out by Mary who, of all Hemingway's wives, was the one who defended his privacy with the most tenacity. There was Martine Carol, whom Hemingway taught to shoot; the Duke and Duchess of Windsor, who were fascinated by the plaster that was peeling off the living room ceiling; Jean-Paul Sartre, who "turned up unexpectedly with a girlfriend and didn't even want the sheets changed";

Antonio Ordoñez, the great torero, who preferred to sunbathe rather than go out fishing on board the *Pilar*; Dominguín, the rival of Ordoñez, less respectful than he, and who criticized Hemingway for his Spanish which he deemed "very mediocre, almost puerile", his immoderate love of alcohol, his machismo bragging and his tactlessness that pushed him to ask too many personal questions about his guest's sex life, especially about his relationship with Ava Gardner.

Dominguín's visit to the *Finca* did not create a good impression on Hemingway. He was not admitted into the sacred circle of real friends with whom Hemingway, as everyone who knew him would agree, was extremely generous. For instance, he helped Luis Quintanilla,

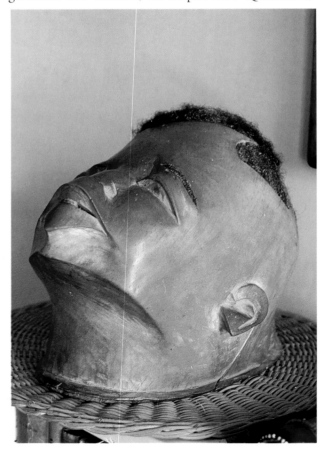

The oval mirror in the guest room called "Venetian room." On the chest of drawers, ritual objects of the Masai tribe.

while he was in prison in Madrid, by financing an exhibition for him at the Pierre-Matisse gallery in New York. This faultless loyalty, Hemingway practiced it without restraint and took great pleasure from it: the novelist Prudencio de Pereda, who was trying to publish his novels, and Ned Calmer, who had applied for a Guggenheim bursary, were both beneficiaries of that generosity. He persuaded Arnold Gingrich to buy paintings from Waldo Pierce and reproduce them in Esquire; he bought paintings by Antonio Gattorno and even published an essay on his work.

At the opposite end of the scale from these real friends there was a constant flow of intruders, journalists, photographers, who hounded Hemingway incessantly. Already in Havana he had to avoid his favorite bars where his admirers would be hanging out waiting for him. On August 25, 1950, he wrote to Robert Cantwell: "This is sort of the pattern. In night clubs people will come up to you and say, 'So you're Hemingway are you?' and swing on you without further explanation. Or they will paw you, which a man doesn't like or start to paw your wife or some girl you know, and if you admonish them, warn them, and then have to clip them, it gets in the papers. Henry James was not faced with these same problems". (*Selected Letters.*) And there was no shortage of bores. In leading position, no doubt, were the rich. He was becoming increasingly hostile towards the jet set, especially those who were part of what was known as the "international" fishing and hunting set. It was to avoid

Martha Gellhorn, in her hotel room in London. She met Hemingway there in May 1944. She was a war correspondent for Time-Life-Fortune and he for Collier's. Eighteen months later she became his third wife, with whom he discovered the *Finca Vigía*. The photograph is by Lee Miller.

them that he left Sun Valley, Bimini and Key West. The diatribe against rich people pronounced by Harry Walden in *The Snows of Kilimanjaro*, was pitiless: they were boring, drank too much, spent their time playing trictrac, and repeating themselves. Hemingway's main criticism of some of his writer friends – John Pale Bishop, Don Stewart, and Scott Fitzgerald – was that they allowed themselves to become awed by the rich man's lifestyle.

Then there were all those he called crazy and bores of all kinds, who even interpreted the Hispano-American warning signs as a kind of challenge, since he had been awarded a certain "Swedish fantasy". One day, it was four young men from some school or other who turned up in the garden of the *Finca* at eleven a.m., while Hemingway had been struggling with his muse since dawn. The next day, a student from New Jersey, a would-be writer, refused to leave the premises until Hemingway agreed to read one of his stories! One morning, he found himself face to face with United States Air force recruits who had won the Aircraftsmen of the month prize: a visit to Hemingway at his home in Cuba! Not to mention the cinema industry that regularly set up their headquarters at the *Finca*, using the phone line, invading the living room and garden! What may seem amusing to some was often experienced by Hemingway, and rightly so, as dramatic: "Interrupting a man who is writing a book is just as shameful as interrupting a man who is in bed making love," he confessed to A. E. Hotchner (*Papa Hemingway*).

But the people Hemingway was the most wary of were incontestably the pretentious intellectuals who filled the ranks of the New York literary circles that he so detested. The *Finca* was regularly visited by commentators, speechifiers, university professors and other journalists, who, if you let them have a square

inch of your skin, would expose you naked at noon in the main square. And make you look as ridiculous as a tragic actor who, in the middle of a solemn tirade, would scratch his butt. Hemingway did not like the book Philip Young wrote, in which he analyzed the writer's work in the light of the traumatic events of his childhood, nor the book by Charles Fenton, a young professor at Yale, which accused him of being a failed author and simultaneously an equally failed FBI agent. Vilified by many of his exegetes, trailed in the mud by literary critics in a hurry, betrayed by his publisher who, after his death, published texts that were cut, altered and re-worked by outsiders, Hemingway hated all this constant flow of intruders

Mary Welsh's room. In the library are books on cookery and gardening, her two passions: *The Tropical Garden, Your Florida Garden, America's Garden Book, French Kitchen, Cook Book,* etc.

Opposite: Directors Chair in brushed oak, which is in fact a copy of an army folding chair.

Right hand page: The garden seen from Mary Welsh's bedroom. She said the main difficulty in gardening in Cuba was to maintain a balance of colours.

work there as long as visitors didn't interrupt their work to the point where we they would have to leave. Life, he said, had been pleasant there for a long time, and life would still be pleasant there if people would leave them alone. He added that they always came back there no matter where they went, and that it was their home. 'And you do not flee your home, you defend it'.

The Hemingways were nonetheless forced to travel a great deal to find the solitude that the writer needed above all else. They had to get away from what Mary called that "perpetual week-end". Between May 1941 and October 1960, they set off on around twenty different trips, taking in Hong Kong, Rangoon, Manila, London, Paris, Genes, New York, Los Angeles, Mombassa, Venice, Cabo Blanco… Summer 1959, during which he went on one of his last trips – to Spain, to watch the bullfighting – was in Hemingway's own opinion one of the best seasons of his life. His last journey was the one that took him by plane from Madrid to New York. But Mary and Ernest Hemingway always went back to the *Finca Vigía*, where they so hated invasions on their privacy. Leicester Hemingway, in his book, *Hemingway, My Brother*, wrote that Hemingway flew into a terrible rage one day when he returned from a fishing trip to find a couple of Leicester's friends that he had invited to stay at the Finca without having taken the trouble to inform Ernest beforehand!

Hemingway's privacy at the *Finca* was primordial, that "haven of rest where neither war nor revolution reached". First of all, there was the staff at the *Finca*, the members of the same crew as the Hemingways, and most of whom had been with the family for a long time. A butler, René Villareal, who, according to Mary Welsh was "energetic, friendly, perfectly aware of his worth, and very devoted to his employers" (who retur-

of all kinds with a vengeance. And so it was hardly surprising when he received Milt Machlin, come to visit Hemingway in September 1958, with invectives like "what the hell are you doing here? Why do you think I came here in the first place? To get away from snoopers like you!" (Argosy, 1958.)

What was Hemingway looking for, if not total immersion in the voluptuous, unique, difficult experience of living? His books are all written talismans to help him to reach his goal. But how could he succeed in this, when undesirables constantly invaded the place he chose to live in? A text he gave to the publication Look, in September 1956, was astonishing and terrible. He said that Mary and he would live and ned the compliment and trusted him implicitly); a chauffeur, Juan, an attractive young Cuban man, in charge of the two cars and the truck, and who also occasionally served as second butler; three gardeners, a carpenter, a caretaker who also looked after the fighting cocks and liked a drink; a neurotic chamber maid, Clara, who had emotional problems and tried to stab the Chinese chef before she was fired; the Chinese chef himself, Ramón – for a short time, he had an assistant called Fico –, who would speak only Chinese and used to come quietly into the dining room and announce to the guests sitting at the table: "There is no lunch today" – he ended up hanging himself from a rusty pipe; and lastly, a mechanic who looked after the boat anchored in the harbor at Cojímar. The house rejoiced in the atmosphere of a circus at times, and Mary had a hard job trying to convince Hemingway that there were other, more organized ways of living, without all the maids, crazy people and sets.

Yes, the *Finca* could be, and for a long time was, a haven of peace. Hemingway loved the mango season, when the mangos were stored in the refrigerator to cool, the season for avocados, the season when the garden produced beautiful healthy vegetables; the lobster season, when he brought back lobster weighing five or six pounds from Cojímar. Life was sweet, at the *Finca*! We can close our eyes and imagine Hemingway standing in his casual indoor clothes, a wide sleeveless guayaberra floating over his khaki shorts. He has thrown off his sandals to go barefoot. He was comfortable in his loose-fitting garments, and touched his shirt where occasionally a little flab was evident. He didn't smoke, he said, in order to preserve his hunter's keen sense of smell. But here we can dispel the myth: he never actually liked cigars!

Certain aspects of life at the *Finca*, when there were no guests staying there, were strictly regulated.

Hemingway coming down
the small stairway leading
from the tower to the
swimming pool. Photograph
taken in 1950.

Until a certain time in the afternoon, no one was allowed to go into the room where Hemingway worked.
When he came out, he would pour himself a drink to
relax before lunch, and he would sometimes read
magazines or newspapers to take his mind off his work.
He didn't say anything; his work had left him too
empty to talk. After lunch, he had a nap. Don't forget
he had been up since five or six a.m. In the early evening, some friends would maybe drop by. But after the
evening meal, he was often already elsewhere.
Thinking of the next day, of the sentence he was going
to finish. The text he was going to continue. If he was
alone, he would put his .22 pistol in his belt, grab his
guiba cane, call Black Dog and take a stroll round the
grounds. If everything was well, he would go back into
the house and go to bed, but not to his own bed, in the
room where he worked, which was covered with
papers, books, various objects and letters; rather, he
would go to sleep with Mary in her room. Such was his
daily routine at the *Finca*. Occasionally, Hemingway
would join in with the chores: he installed a roan pipe
to collect the rainwater. At other times, he would look
after his son who was ill, take care of him, and put a
camp bed beside his bed so that the child would be at

his side all through the night.

The *Finca* was also the scene of dramas, especially
marital scenes. Quarrels, marital problems. Married
four times, Hemingway divorced three times: Hadley,
Pauline, Martha, and Mary. What were his female
conquests really? What kind of relationship did he have
with women? Many of the women who turned against
him did it because they were disappointed and felt
cheated by false promises. Was Hemingway misun-
derstood and incapable of affection? Who knows? One
day, he did confide in his friend Marlene Dietrich that
there was no hidden meaning in his books, no symbolism, and that he avoided being sentimental. Hunters
couldn't afford to be sentimental. Animals mate
without any subtle emotions. No sweet sighing during
intercourse! To hell with social subtleties! Men eat
women. Women eat men. (Quoted by Jeffrey Meyers,
in *Hemingway*). Hemingway always married the same
type of woman. On the one hand, he boasted that he
always managed to find good wives, and on the other
hand, he deplored the fact that he was stupid as far as
women were concerned, because he always felt he had
to marry them. Rare were the women who were able to
stand up to this grumpy colossus used to total adora-
tion and complete freedom. Mary tried, criticizing his
lack of hygiene, his cowardice, his excessive drinking,
and his vulgar language. She went against his will by
having his cat Boise castrated and having the roots of
the ceiba cut. Hemingway gave an affectionate if
somewhat curious description of her in a magazine
article published in Look, in September 1956, which
stated that when Mary wasn't here, the *Finca* was as
empty as the emptiest of bottles that Mary had ever
had removed and he lived in emptiness as solitary as
the light on a radio when the batteries are flat and there
is no socket to plug it into to.

It was during a trip to Venice, in 1948, that

The childrens room, which later became a second guest room. Ingrid Bergman, Gary Cooper, Ava Gardner, Errol Flynn, Rocky Marciano, Jean-Paul Sartre and Dominguín all slept there at one time or another.

Hemingway met the woman who was to become Renata in '*Across the River and Into the Trees*'. Adriana Ivancich was an Italian noblewoman and was Hemingway's last love, even though the relationship was purely platonic. He loved to be in her company and to talk to her; there was no doubt she got his creative juices flowing once more. Without her, he would never have written '*Across the River and Into the Trees*', and perhaps he would never have finished *The Old Man and the Sea*. The little countess who had lost her fortune almost came between Hemingway and his wife. Adriana came with her mother to the *Finca* in the autumn of 1950. The White Tower came in useful once more, for Hemingway and Adriana would often go there together to "work" on the setting up of a tem-

porary association that was to be called "the limited company". But their relationship, as Adriana later said, was purely platonic. Mary stood her ground. She said she would stay and look after Hemingway's house and the *Finca* until the day that he came there, sober, one morning and told her truly and clearly that he wanted her to leave. (J. R. Mellow, *Hemingway*.) Adriana went back to Venice, published her autobiography, *The White Tower*, married a German Count, left him, fell victim to depression and alcohol, and hanged herself from a tree north of Rome in 1983.

It is widely accepted that women are absent from the American novel. As far as Hemingway is concerned, while it is true that the only story he wrote from a woman's point of view was a short story, *A Cat in the*

FOLLOWING PAGE: The Tower of the *Finca Vigía*. Built in 1947 to a plan drawn by Mary Welsh. Ground floor: bathroom WC. First floor: the cat-house. Second floor: armoury. Third floor: military library and study. Hemingway hardly ever worked there and gradually let the cats become masters of the place.

Rain, composed in Rapallo in May 1923, his work is not that of a world of men without women. Women are omnipresent, and constantly play their part. A just reflection of the life of Hemingway in which women played such a major role. Capable of proclaiming that American women were the hardest in the world, the most greedy and the most seductive, his character Thomas Hudson, in *Islands in the Stream*, says: "I've been very happy with women. Desperately happy. Unbearably happy. So happy that I could not believe it; that it was like being drunk or crazy". Was Hemingway thinking of Adriana when he concluded his last major book, '*Across the River and Into the Trees*', with the terrible thought that lovers were what they were, a little happier than other people, then one of them feels emptiness for ever?

This is the emptiness we feel when walking through the rooms of this house that is now a museum. It has been arrested in time, and is now fixed and static. We can try to imagine what Hemingway's departure from here must have been like. A life that suddenly stops. Here is his hat, here his cane; the emblem of the *Finca* embroidered on a napkin. On the cutlery, three mountains, Montparnasse, Montmartre and Sainte-Geneviève. The three mountains of Paris and the three hills around the *Finca*. An arrowhead; that of the Ojibway tribe. Its territory was that of little Ernest's childhood, Michigan and Minnesota. As for the horizontal lines, they stand for the rank of Captain, which was the rank, both Mary Welsh and Hemingway held during the Second World War. The *Finca* fades into the background. We can hear Mary's voice saying "I think living in sin is marvelous". Hemingway's voice muttering that he needs his wife in my bed, not in magazines with wide circulations! Ghosts, fragments of the time that has elapsed since the house was inhabited. Unfinished manuscripts left in the strongbox at the bank: *A Moveable Feast, Islands in the Stream,* started in 1946 and abandoned in 1951... then the departure from the *Finca.* On April 1st, 1960, Hemingway could still write from the *Finca Vigía* that water in the swimming pool was just right. But very soon after the failed landing at the Bay of Pigs, the Cuban government took over the *Finca Vigía.* Luckily, Miró's *The Farm* was no longer there; it was on loan to the Modern Art Museum in New York. Hemingway felt severed when he had to leave Cuba. On November 30, 1960, he was admitted to the Mayo clinic in Rochester, then, under the name of George Saviers, he was moved to St. Mary's Hospital. He was depressed and defeated. He sent a letter to his literary director that should have sounded warning bells, saying that things had been

tough and were tough everywhere – the situation in Cuba – no libraries for working, etc. Hemingway knew he would never return to San Francisco de Paula. A. E. Hotchner suggests that in addition to this final break, he also constructed three other walls, the walls of his new prison: he could not return to Rochester, he could not go back to his New York apartment, and he could not go back to Ketchum. He was being followed, pursued, and was receiving threats. He couldn't write any more, and spent his time, emptied, impotent, in front of the manuscript of *A Moveable Feast,* without being able to work on it.

Time went by. In July 1964, Mary wrote to Juan Pastor, the former chauffeur, that in New York, with the heat, she missed the *Finca* enormously and also

Adriana Ivancich. Hemingway met the young Venetian aristocrat at Latisana, in November 1948. She came to the *Finca.* And he fell in love with her. She gave him the strength to press on with *The Old Man and the Sea* (he wrote it during her visit) and revive *Across the River and Into the Trees.* "In the beginning, this man who spoke slowly and incomprehensibly bored me a little. He is so much older than me and has so much more experience of life! But I think he likes to have me by his side and talk and talk" (Epoca.)

The fourth floor of the tower Hemingway and Adriana Ivancich met there often.

Beside the pool; The graves
of Hemingway's four dogs:
Blackdog, Negrita, Linda
and Neron.

Ernest Hemingway and his
chauffeur Juan Pastor.

mentioned the good life they had there. Boise, the cat
that belonged to Thomas Hudson and to Ernest
Hemingway, died at the *Finca* in 1966. The staff,
faithful to the custom, wrapped him in a sheet and
buried him at the foot of the dining room door. Time
went by. Several years later, Mary Welsh obtained
authorization from the Cuban government to take to
the United States the works of art that had remained
at the *Finca*, as well as a number of manuscripts and
copious correspondence. But the ghosts were already
there, and the memories, the sacrileges. In 1962, only
a year after Hemingway's death, the Cuban artillery
was deployed in the garden of the *Finca Vigía*: this was
at the time of the soviet missile crisis. Then silence,
once more. A cat appeared from nowhere, stretched,
yawned, then lay down on the foot of the writer, of the
writer's ghost, and stayed there. Again, the voice of
Hemingway, off-stage, like in the cinema, repeating
haunting phrases, in a hurry to get back to work.
Today, the fifty year old ceiba, which had hardly any
leaves, has been replaced by a smaller one: it was threatening to cause irreparable damage to the house. A
ceiba, a few feet tall, for a new life, without
Hemingway this time, and whose roots will perhaps
one day push up the paving stones on the patio. In the
meantime, another era descended on Cuba. The era of

the blockade, with monthly rations of meat, fish, chicken, rice, pork fat, beans, butter, and eggs that were
reduced every day. Cuba had nothing left. There was
no detergent, no pens, no soap, no paper, many hou-
seholds and some public establishments had no drinking water. Three centuries apart, the Cubans relived
the drama of the population of *Cartagena de Indias*,
besieged by a hundred and twenty British Navy ves-
sels. Our sense of history forbids us to think that history is repeating itself. There is still time. On his *ecu*,
Laurent de Médicis had a vertiginous motto inscribed:
"Time returns". Yes, no doubt. And so too, a letter,
sent by Hemingway from the *Finca*, on April 15,
1948, to General Charles T. Lanham. It ended with
these words so full of humor, grandeur and exactitude,
that say it all about writing and Cuba: "Moi écrivain
de San Francisco de Paula. Moi écrire des bouquins.
Moi pense jamais." (*Selected Letters.*)

The London Sunday Times published an article on December 19, 1954 in which Mary Welsh wrote that the average English gardener couldn't imagine the fatigue, hard work and stubbornness a tropical garden demands. But it was worth the trouble, for the rich shades of green are a magnificent background for the bright hues of the hibiscus and the bougainvilleas. In the rambling landscape of hills, she added, the *Finca Vigía* was an oasis of coolness and beauty.

The Fishing Chair of the *Pilar*,
a 38-foot motor boat which
left the Brooklyn shipyard
on May 9, 1934.

Beyond the Great Blue River

Hemingway posing with one of his catches. Marlins and swordfish can weigh up to 500lb.

Even though I am not a believer in the Analysis, I spend a hell of a lot of time killing animals and fish so I won't kill myself. When a man is in rebellion against death, as I am in rebellion against death, he gets pleasure out of taking to himself one of the godlike attributes, that of giving it.

CONFIDED BY ERNEST HEMINGWAY TO AVA GARDNER.
Quoted by A. E. Hotchner in *Papa Hemingway.*

When trying to discuss Hemingway in the light of Hegel, Georges Bataille claims that the confrontation with death enables the man he calls the "master" to extract the value and essence from human life. He goes on to add: "Fishing, and particularly hunting, have always been games, often the privilege of the masters." But what can we say when this privilege derives from childhood, is nothing more than a way of being, a family habit? Later, when Hemingway had grown up to be a man and a writer, he would create a character, a young hero whom he was to call Nick Adams and who, like himself, was perhaps seeking a diversion from his existential anguish through fishing and hunting. But we haven't yet reached this stage. Ernest Hemingway is a child, born in a wooden framed house at 439 North Oak Park Avenue in a Chicago suburb. His mother, Grace Hall, a soloist in the First Congregationist Church choir, loved music

and religion and was to give the names of saints to her daughters. His father, Clarence Edmunds Hemingway, a member of the same church, was a respected doctor but, unlike his wife, he was a keen hunter, "more proud of the pheasant and deer that he brought down with a sure shot," say the Hemingway exegetes, "than of the patients he saved from death". Ernest received his first fishing rod for his third birthday. His mother offered him a cello for his eighth bir-

Morro lighthouse, at the entrance to the Bay of Havana *Le Castillo de los Tres Reyes del Morro* was completed in 1630. The Tower of Morro became a lighthouse in 1764. Rebuilt in 1844 under the orders of Captain, General Leopoldo O'Donnell, the lighthouse was electrified in 1945.

thday and his paternal grandfather gave him his first 20 rifle just after he reached the age of eleven.

The Hemingway family had two houses. One respectable and distinguished: fifteen rooms, including a music room, all impregnated with the Victorian and Puritan values of America at the time. The second house was at Hortons Bay, in the state of Michigan, on the banks of Lake Walloon. Hemingway was to spend every summer there until the age of seventeen, and after the 1914 war he would return there to forget the horror and start his career as a writer. It was here, in the family's roughly built cedar-wood chalet, between a sawmill on the outskirts of a small town and the village of the Ojibway Indians, peace-loving foresters of the Algonquin people, that Hemingway reveled in untamed nature, learning about the nature of existence and the cruelty of nature. For the young Ernest

this valley was a veritable paradise. He could run barefoot among the trees, fish and swim in the lake with his father, light campfires, flush out birds and gather wild flowers. At the age of five he was already able to accompany his father on long hikes of more than ten kilometers, from which he would return with bleeding feet, but fortified and happy. Hemingway was to be marked forever by this immense natural universe, by this virgin and authentic world. He always felt an extreme repugnance for cities. Hunting and fishing were often to figure, throughout his work (and life) as a constant: "The happiest day I ever had was any day when I woke in the morning when I was a boy and I did not have to go to school or to work. In the morning I was always hungry when I woke and I could smell the dew in the grass and hear the wind in the high branches of the hemlock trees, if there was a

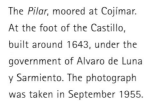

The *Pilar*, moored at Cojímar. At the foot of the Castillo, built around 1643, under the government of Alvaro de Luna y Sarmiento. The photograph was taken in September 1955.

wind, and if there was no wind I could hear the quietness of the forest and the calmness of the lake and I would listen for the first noises of morning. Sometimes the first noise would be a kingfisher flying over the water that was so calm it mirrored his reflection and he made a clattering cry as he flew. Sometimes it would be a squirrel chittering in one of the trees outside the house, his tail jerking each time he made a noise. Often it would be the plover calling on the hillside." (*Islands in the Stream.*)

He would pursue this paradise lost throughout his life. In the 1920s many of the first texts he sent to the Toronto Daily Star or the Toronto Star Weekly spoke of fishing and prefigured the move to Key West, then Cuba. In them he described trout fishing with its stunning flies, fishing for long and slim mackerel, massive bass, silver and slate-blue tuna. For this kind of fishing along the Spanish coast he already evoked the struggle between man and fish, "physically tough and backbreaking work" that guarantees you, in the case of victory, the certitude of a purification – then you would be admitted without any difficulty before the most ancient gods, and they would welcome you. This struggle with the animal world, which we again find in Nick Adams, has something of the struggle between innocence and experience, the background of Huck Finn, Mark Twain's famous hero. On the one hand, the pure and idealized world of childhood; on the other, that of the adult man, a world of disillusion and horror. From the Big Two-Hearted River to the Gulf Stream there is only one step, or one life, whichever we choose, but which ends in fiction with a head resting on a left arm, an open razor on the blankets, the blade open to the air – (*The Nick Adams Stories*) and, in reality, with a gunshot ringing through a sleeping house on the morning of July 2nd 1961.

A few more words about the Big Two-Hearted

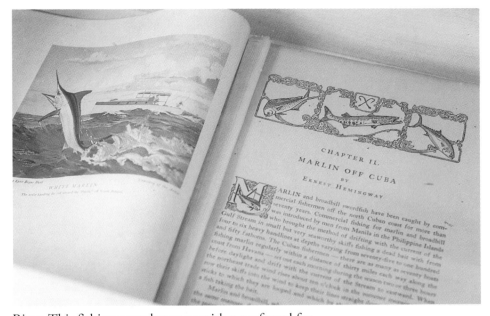

River. This fishing story leaves us with a profound feeling of tragedy, an everyday drama, an impression of mystery that seems to hide behind the appearance of a banal short story. Yes, a fishing story, with all that water acting as an immense vehicle for anguish and pain. The Gulf Stream only deepens, accentuates this tension: on the one hand, the smoothest of surfaces; on the other, the depths with their hidden, threatening intentions. Cuban fishermen call this marine region the Great Well "because", as Santiago reminds us in *The Old Man and the Sea*, "there was a sudden deep of seven hundred fathoms where all sorts of fish congregated because of the swirl the current made against the steep walls of the floor of the ocean." It was contained within bands of milky yellow seaweed stretching in banks as far as the eye could see and circled by busy birds following the shoals of tuna. Who could resist the evil charm of this sea current that is still one of the last wild places on earth? Here, "the sea is exactly the same as it was before men came with their boats"; here, "when you let yourself go with the cur-

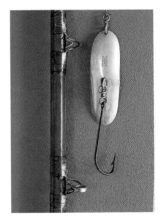

Fishing hooks and rods exhibited in room 525 of the hotel Ambos Mundos, now a museum.

Top: In the tower, illustrated edition of *La pesca de la aguja en las costas de Cuba*, published by Denydale Press.

rent, out of sight of the coast, watching your four lines of sixty, eighty, a hundred and a hundred and fifty fathoms, and that on depths of seven hundred fathoms, you never know what might seize the small tuna you're using as bait" ("On the Blue Water", *Esquire*, 1933). Floating on this river that carries you along with the flow, life takes on another meaning. Everything seems far away, beginning with the Cuban coast, and you think of beautiful or unfortunate things, personal memories, lies, secret motivations until the angle of the light, or the clicking of the slowly unwinding reel, or the sudden tautening of a slack line brings you back to Hemingway, whom you are not, but whom, for a few moments, you thought you were. But let's get on to the *Pilar*, a floating myth…

As Norberto Fuentes suggests, there comes a time in the life of a fisherman when he wants to practice his art on his own boat. When Hemingway returned from a trip to Europe in 1934 he sent photos and accounts of his African expedition to Esquire magazine. Gringrich advanced him $3,000 (of the $7,500 he

asked for), which allowed him to order the Wheeler Shipyard in Brooklyn to build a boat he christened with the name *Pilar* (*Nuestra Señora del Pilar*, "Our Lady of the Pillar"), in honor of the portrait of the Virgin in the church at Sargasso, of the *feria* that takes place in October to celebrate the same Virgin, and of Pauline who had chosen this nickname when she fell in love with Hemingway. Thirty-eight feet long and twelve across, made of cedar and white oak, it had a green bridge, a black hull and a pilothouse made of varnished mahogany. It was fitted with two engines, one seventy-five horsepower and the other forty, two propellers and a double rudder. The *Pilar* went to Miami by train on May 12, 1934. Hemingway was waiting for it and baptized it with a bottle of champagne. From then on the writer would spend hours on his boat sailing back and forth an incalculable number of times over the waters separating Havana from *Cayo Paraiso*, then setting out on interminable fishing trips from Cojímar, his Cuban home-port.

Situated a few miles to the east of Havana, originally only a small village "with low houses stretching out both sides of a bay, where the men fished in their small individual boats fitted with sails and oars"

The interior of the *Pilar*.
She could sleep eight people;
six in the cabin and two in
the pilot's house.

The pilot's house of the *Pilar*, all in varnished mahogany. The boat had two engines giving 65 and 40 horse power respectively.

(Jeffrey Meyer, *Hemingway*), Cojímar has become one of the legendary sailing spots in the Gulf Stream. In the bar of the La Terraza restaurant Hemingway rubbed shoulders with his fishermen friends and peasants from the inlands, non-communicative men, and shy except when they had taken drink. It was here, close to the counter built on the rocks overlooking the port, that Thomas Hudson saw Boise the cat for the first time, which he would finally adopt, and it was here that he looked at the brown and gnarled hands of the old fishermen, that were sunburnt scarred and stitched. It was here that Hemingway wanted to film the location shots for the film adaptation of *The Old Man and the Sea*. But it was impossible. In 1956, the expansion of Havana to the east forced him to look for ano-

ther fishing port on the north coast. Today the Cojímar that Hemingway knew no longer exists. Souvenir shops have replaced the original little port: Hemingway square with its belvedere and bust of the writer, and Gregorio Fuentes, a living witness seated at a table of La Terraza, speaking, for a few dollars, of times gone by.

However, the road that leads to Cojímar is still the same, with its hens' nests and rare automobiles. The sea is still the same, full of smells and wind, spray and fishing birds, and the fish still cross the deep waters of the Gulf Stream. Hemingway's first big catch dates from 1933, a four hundred and sixty pound swordfish. It took him a little over an hour to hoist it up to the spar. Deep-sea fishing is a sport and a mystique. It

FOLLOWING DOUBLE PAGE:
Hemingway wrote in Holiday, July 1949, that when people asked him why he lived in Cuba he would tell them the main reason was the big bright blue river three quarters of a mile to a mile deep and sixty to eighty miles wide, that was just a minute from the door of his house across beautiful countryside, and which, in calm conditions, provided the best fishing he had ever known.

was Joe "Grunts" Russell who, on board the *Anita*, initiated Hemingway into this strange sport: struggling with a sea monster, sometimes for several hours, and getting it out of the water as quickly as possible before the sharks have time to devour it. To the sound of the undulating flying fish with the plover-waders diving into the waves to seize them in full flight, the barracudas and groupers flashing their shadows through the long, smooth rolling of the groundswell, the swordfish buckle and dive, the marlin shining like quicksilver, trouble the slow movements of the water, slicing into it like scythes, opening breaches, crossing and recrossing the lines as they turn and swirl. Fishing can lead to strange feats of strength. In 1935, Hemingway caught the biggest marlin ever hooked in the Atlantic:

it weighed one hundred and nineteen pounds. Another year he got the better of a seven hundred and eighty nine pound blue shark. All these records are officially listed. Writing is a serious business, so is fishing . Hemingway was one of the first to perfect a fishing technique that consists of bringing large tuna close to the boat as quickly as possible so that they still have the strength, while engaged in a struggle with the fisherman, to avoid the teeth of the sharks. One day he took out some marine biologists from the Philadelphia Academy of Science who had come to study the habits of swordfish. Hemingway introduced them to a previously unlisted species. They immediately named it "Neomarinthe Hemingway".

Hemingway was a real fisherman, keen and tena-

Hemingway at the *Finca* with his fishing buddies: el Sordo, Cachimba, Cheo Lopez, Arsenio Ova Carnero, Gregorio Fuentes, Tato and Quintin.

cious, and it is hardly surprising that in 1950 a fishing competition was named after him, for which he devised some of the regulations. Hemingway was a professional who could deliver a masterly discourse on deepsea fishing any time. Leonard Lyons of the New York Post reported in his article of June 26, 1953: "Hemingway is peremptory: – The only thing you have to watch is the vibrating of the boat. Watch that constantly. If you can hear it, you can be sure that the fish, even ninety feet down, can also hear it. There's no chance it'll approach."

Fishing is a strange and serious business. Losing can become a victory. According to Hemingway, one of the most exciting events in his life was the legendary fishing expedition he undertook in May 1935 off Key West. On May 23, at the end of the afternoon, he landed the biggest basking shark ever caught from a boat with rod and reel. The catch however, was not recorded. It was not the same person who hooked the fish, who actually hoisted it on board. But what inexpressible joy there must have been behind this unlisted record!

Fishing is just as important as writing. The gestation of a novel is nobody's business but the author's, said Hemingway, who didn't like talking about his work with the journalists who came to interview him. When one of them asked whether he didn't speak more readily about fishing, his response was unequivocal. He said that as far back as he could remember, he always adored fishing. And that's another thing he didn't much like to discuss except with people for whom it's their main activity, professional fishermen. (New York Times Book Review, September 7 1952.)

What about the ocean? Hemingway didn't want it to be made into a hostile force. He compared it to a prostitute that one cannot really love but for whom one feels a lot of affection and whom one continues to see, "*La puta mar* that we have loved and that has clapped us all and poxed us too" (*Selected Letters*, to Bernard Berenson, 13 September 1952). But the great question running through this constantly renewed water is its mystery, what it hides, what it delivers up or keeps. Hemingway, who was a great hunter, poses an interesting question for his readers in Esquire. When hunting, he writes, you always know what you're looking for and the largest prize is an elephant. But who could tell what may nibble at your hook when you let it drift down in the Gulf Stream to a depth of one hundred and fifty fathoms? It is true that hunting does not have these same hidden depths.

But here again, childhood is present. In an article he published in Esquire in February 1935, Hemingway asked if we could remember the first woodcock we shot while walking in the prairie with our father? Where does literature come from? For Hemingway, perhaps it comes from this childhood place of fishing and hunting. Compared to his African wanderings during which he encountered lions, antelopes, elephants, rhinoceroses; compared to his mountain hunting, autumns with snow and brown and gold leaves where he could find prey like elk, deer, wild mouflon sheep and bears, compared to these, Cuba, with its plains, mountains and *Pinar del Río* tobacco fields could hardly offer him more than the odd duck and rare deer, which were becoming rapidly extinct. All that was left for him then, in order to satisfy his thirst for cartridges and tracking, was the flying or clay pigeons of the Cazadores del Cerro Club. Situated in the Cerro district, this club enabled him to frequent the Creole aristocracy, wealthy Cubans and rich Americans. The big game hunter was reduced to shooting with a double barrel Remington. But the club pleased at least one person, Hemingway's son, Gregory H., who enjoyed the distinction of beating Batista's

chief of police in a competition. As Robert Escarpit very well understood, there was "a curious dialectic of fishing and hunting" in this man who didn't like killing animals, who asked his sons when they picked up a wounded duck in the course of a hunt to wring its neck as quickly as possible in order to prevent it from suffering, and who was capable of treating a wounded owl for weeks. Fishing, like hunting, transformed into new literary symbols, acquired a metaphysical dimension and between them constituted a metaphor of life, of hope, and of death. There is neither indifference nor distance in them. The hunter and fisherman, in their locked battle with the animal, are tracking emotion, give themselves up to it and never come out of it except as victor or vanquished.

The line and the rifle only extend the man's action, they do not cut him off in anyway from his fear or anguish. As for the *Pilar*, it constitutes the focal point from which the and ups and downs and leitmotifs of a life radiated.

Thus life went by on the *Pilar*, in the confined space of its three separate compartments with an odor of tar and oakum floating in the air. In the first, installed under the foredeck, two berths and a table; in the second, the galley and the toilet; in the third, another berth, along with a space reserved for supplies and ruled over by Gregorio Fuentes, sailor on board the *Pilar* since 1938. Life in this confined space, which inspired the writer with many tales, articles, images and sensations, was permeated with fishing and friendship. When the *Pilar* leaves the gray-green waters of the port and its bow cuts into the dark blue sea, the days roll on, always the same, an always changing. They prepare bait, cero mackerel or moonfish. They check that the Hatuey beer is cool. When the boat drops anchor, and after a salutary bath, they have a hot meal with a main course of freshly caught fish and avocado seasoned with mustard vinaigrette. From the top of his pilothouse and from the flying bridge from which four powerful lines can be cast simultaneously, Hemingway gives the orders, breathing in the sea air in search of the edge of the Gulf Stream. Gregorio Fuentes follows the fishing: "Fish! Fish!" or: "A bite! A bite!"

Life on the *Pilar* is, just like life at the *Finca*, a mixture of order and chaos. Some days, when the old gramophone deigned to work, they would play records: Listening to Stormy Weather, High Wind; or perhaps a sketch by Jimmy Durante wearing himself out explaining how to hypnotize boas. Hemingway's brother, Leicester, reports good-humoredly that these recordings had finally become so unbearable that the

guests and the crew plotted the destruction of the obsessive records. But Ernest cherished them too much and his eye was too sharp for them to be able to get rid of them purely and simply by throwing them overboard. (*Hemingway, My Brother*).

Hemingway, who knew how dangerous the sun could be in the Caribbean, put several layers of folded paper serviettes on his head and had himself regularly sprayed with salt water; sometimes he personally made sure that everyone had their faces coated with a zinc oxide ointment.

Fights were inevitable. A fisherman's pride is a touchy question. Joseph Knapp, a highly respected publisher who dared to doubt the authenticity of Hemingway's fishing stories did so at his own expense. The argument took on unexpected proportions. "Slug, sonofabitch," jabbed Knapp, receiving as his only response two left hooks. End of argument, and of fight…

In spite of a few rare bores who disturbed life on board, like the Shevlin couple who considered the

Pilar to be tiny and the existence to be had there "perfectly odious," the atmosphere was pretty cheerful. Hemingway's fishing friends, a small group of a half dozen individuals, some of whom were helped financially when they were in need, were not intellectuals. To his sea-faring life Hemingway applied the "anti-intellectual" tradition of the great American literature of the inter-war period. Thus, the poet Archibald MacLeish, having embarked on the *Pilar*, was abandoned on an uninhabited island between Boca Grande and Snipe Keys on the excuse that he frightened the fish. He owed his rescue to Pauline, but gained a nickname: "the Robinson Crusoe of American poetry". The real geniuses allowed to walk the decks of the *Pilar* were neither millionaires nor intellectuals. Their names were José Luis Herrera, Sinsky, aka Sinbad the sailor, Don Andrés and a few others, all fishermen, "sons of death", like Carlos Gutiérrez, the "king of skippers". Hemingway loved nothing so much as simple and ordinary people, singers in bars, thugs, smugglers, cock breeders, pelota and baseball players, veterans of the Spanish Civil War, soldiers, a motley cohort, cheerful and boisterous, hunters, delivery boys… When he received the Pulitzer Prize on May 4, 1953 for *The Old Man and the Sea*, he learnt the news by radio on board the *Pilar*! And when, one year later, he was awarded the Nobel Prize, his first thoughts were for his fishermen friends. He said that the prize belonged to Cuba because his work was conceived and created in Cuba, with the people of Cojímar, of which he was a citizen. And we know that he was to donate the Swedish award as a gift to the chapel of Virgen de la Caridad del Cobre: In *Hemingway, My Brother*, he is quoted as saying "We never really own something until we give it away."

When Hemingway lived at Key West he sometimes went to sea for several months and fished every

Santa Cruz del Norte, between Tijeras and Pta. Escondido, to the east of Cojímar. Hemingway and Joe Russell came from Key West for bottles of Rón Yucayo which they smuggled back.

In *By Line*, Hemingway wrote that once you had left behind the coast and the other boats, you were more alone than you could ever be hunting, and the sea was exactly the same as it had been before men came with their boats.

day from sunrise to sunset. After he went to live at the *Finca* he could fish when he wanted and continue to explore Cuba and the surrounding seas. His excursions took him as far as the cayos of the Sabana-Camagüey archipelago and Nuevitas, essentially between 1940 and 1950: Cayo Frances, Cayo Media Luna, Cayo Guillermo, Cayo Paredon Grande, Cayo Anton, Cayo Confites, and Cayo Verde. He would sail to the east of Havana, toward *Jaimanitas, Palaya Baracoa, El Solado, Puerta Banes, Mariel, Cabans, Bahia Honda, La Mulata,* not far from *Cayo Paraíso*. Or, navigating to the west, would come across Becurango, Tarará, *El Mégano, Santa Cruz del Norte,* or *Puerto Escondido,* where a famous photo shows him reading in the water and wearing a hat of woven palm leaves like the peasants and fishermen of the island.

When he wasn't sailing on the deep waters of the *puta mar* Hemingway gave himself up to his favorite pastime: exalting virility. Here again, references to childhood and the values he learned on the open territory around Walloon Lake were second nature. Hemingway learnt to box at the age of fourteen. In his very first match his partner, a professional boxer, broke his nose. A few weeks later an eye wound led to a partial, definitive loss of sight in one eye. The love of physical exercise, risks, exertion, all these were sacred to him and we find them throughout his life in varied and violent virile practices: baseball, the Cuban national sport, cock fighting, a great Havanese spectacle, tennis (he was a member of the very select Veda do

In an article published in Esquire in the autumn of 1933, Hemingway described fishing off the Morro, with the cooling breeze and the small boats of the marlin fishers spread out as far as the eye can see. They fished with four to six lines at a depth of forty to seventy fathoms, letting their lines drift freely to catch the fish swimming in the depths.

Tennis Club), bull fighting, jai alai, American football:

"Lives of football men remind us,
We can dive and kick and slug,
And departing leave behind us,
Hoof prints on another's mug."

(Poem written at Oak Park in 1986, *88 poems*).

Childhood again, in the knocks received, the wounds, the accidents that incessantly punctuated Hemingway's life. His brother recounts that when Ernest was about ten years old he ran to fetch a milk bucket with a stick in his hand. He tripped, the stick perforated the back of his throat, almost completely exposing his tonsils. The child lost a lot of blood but managed to make his way home. His father, a doctor, was there to stop the bleeding. In the course of his life, with the exception of illness, Hemingway met with some thirty-odd more or less serious accidents: cere-

PREVIOUS DOUBLE PAGE: In *Esquire*
(1934) Hemingway wrote that
"when the northeast wind
blows against the current the
sea swells, and you can only
fish across the swell, but you
have to go in the direction
of it or mount it."

OPPOSITE: The *Pilar* at sea.
Hemingway wrote in the
review Holiday (July 1949)
that the *Pilar* had been built
as a fishing boat, and to be
sturdy in rough weather,
with cruising autonomy of at
least five hundred miles.

bral concussion, burns, cuts, fractures, etc. A unique fighter, perfectly in tune with his time, he received an incalculable number of blows and finally learned to give as good as he got.

Of course he belongs to what we might call a "line" of virile writers, from Balzac to Stendhal, Dostoyevsky to Mark Twain, Victor Hugo to Chesterton. Of course he is capable of refusing to wear a coat in the middle of winter because he hates it, for why should we get all wrapped up merely because it's a little chilly? But at heart, sport, boxing, and the fascination with violence, were more a question of morality and philosophy. Rather than being able to hit hard, it was essential to be able to take the knocks without complaining. Examples are the wounded toreador in the arena in

For Whom the Bell Tolls; the professional boxer capable of taking blows and losing a fixed match; the fisherman who hooks a magnificent fish and loses it. In violence we learn defeat. Hemingway liked primitive, violent people, because they told him about himself. In 1954, he confided to Kurt Singer in the Washington Post that we were all in the ring, that we survive only if we fight, and he was always ready to put on the gloves. Of course he still boxed, and said he would box until his last day and on that day he would box against himself to accept death as something beautiful, the same beauty that we see Sunday after Sunday in the arenas. When he gave up the ghost, he went on, the crowd would contemplate him with the same detached interest as whores when they look at a

Hart Crane, William Faulkner, Dashiell Hammett, Sinclair Lewis, Jack London, John O'Hara, Eugene O'Neill, John Steinbeck were none of them members of the temperance leagues! So, yes, Hemingway drank. Pints of alcohol – essentially very strong martini gins, fifteen parts gin for one part vermouth, a lot of beer and champagne. And improbable cocktails at the Floridita. Gregorio Fuentes made a list of the alcoholic combinations drunk on board the Pilar: tonics (gin, water, lemon, never sugar), whisky soda (White Label, Haig and Haig, Johnny Walker), Italian, Chilean and Spanish wines, daiquiris (without sugar), Bacardi rum (with ice and lemon). When the *Pilar* left Havana bay and sailed past the Morro, Hemingway would pronounce the magic words that Captain Grigorine was responsible for the alcohol department. The list goes on. Once they were back on land the drinking continued: whisky, gin, Campari, Rón Collins, tequila, French rosé, Chianti. Norberto Fuentes recalls "four or five bottles with each meal"! Anecdotes abound. Lanham recounts that in spite of a massive dose of sleeping pills, Hemingway always woke up at about half past four in the morning, immediately started drinking and sat down to write, "a pen in one hand and a glass in the other" (Jeffrey Meyers, *Hemingway*). A witness at the Floridita states that Hemingway, having drunk a good ten bottles,

The *Pilar* was purchased from Wheeler Shipyard, in Brooklyn, for the sum of three thousand dollars.

bull. And here we have another clue – the myth of physical invincibility is the misleading legend behind which a stoic Hemingway hides: victory through defeat, thanks to bravery and faith.

The man the Vorarlberg mountaineers nicknamed "the black, kirsch-drinking Christ" is a wounded man who sees alcohol as an essential attribute of virility. At least this is what one might think. A man who cannot "hold" drink is not a man. He reproaches people with not being able to hold their liquor, Scott Fitzgerald for falling into a drunken stupor on one glass of champagne, Primo Carnera, Tom Wolfe who would drown in a thimbleful of whisky. It has been written that he drank to forget that his talent had run dry. This is, of course, debatable. James Agee, Raymond Chandler,

HYPOPRION BREVIROSTRIS   *Poey*

2.00 ᴛᴏ 2.60 ᴹ

TIBURÓN GALANO

The Tiburon Galano. This plate is an excerpt from the famous book by Carlos de la Torre y Huerta: Fishes of Cuba and the Atlantic Coasts of Tropical America. "He had sailed for two hours (...) when he saw the first of the two sharks. "*Galanos*", he said aloud. He had seen the second fin now coming up behind the first."

(*The Old Man and the Sea*.)

requested a double rum with Coca-Cola. Which surprised the barman. Hemingway seemingly answered "Because I didn't have any breakfast this morning!" In the large living room at the *Finca Vigía* there was a cocktail bar table Hemingway designed himself specially to allow himself to grasp the bottles by the neck without getting up from his armchair! In the beautiful book he devotes to Hemingway, Robert Escarpit points out how much wine is a part of the natural setting of his novels. His America was the America of Prohibition whisky; his Switzerland that of Valais white wine; his Italy that of marsala and the red wines of the Pô plain; his Spain that of beer and anis del Toro; his France that of Pernod, referred to as that pale

The bust of Ernest Hemingway erected at Cojímar by his fishing companions. The date of birth is wrong. Hemingway was born on July 21, 1899, at Oak Park, a small puritanical town near Chicago.

imitation of absinthe that gives you a whiplash like whisky, but immediately lets you drop, and, lastly absinthe, which plays a major role in *For Whom the Bell Tolls.*

Drink, like tongues, speaks to us of forgotten memories, but even more important, it helps bring oblivion and to make the unbearable bearable. The old drunk in the story called "A Clean, Well-Lighted Place" gets drunk, he says, through despair, but especially for no reason, as he was later to kill himself, for no reason. Hemingway often talked about alcohol in interviews and in his books. In *Death in the Afternoon* he wrote that the bottle was a means of acting, a sovereign means; if you don't want to use it as a projectile, you can always drink it. Thomas Hudson, in *Islands in the Stream*, confesses to himself "You're always drinking against something or for something now."

Just like violence, alcohol is a mask. By serving the legend it protects Hemingway and joins the panoply of the larger-than-life big game hunter, the war correspondent, the tough slayer of sea monsters, the wild man, the insatiably visceral, power incarnate, monument to virility, chimera with a thousand faces that are not him and constitute an image that protects him, which he does not deign complete and which he complains about. As he writes in a letter, he wanted to be known as a writer; not as a man who had been through several wars; and not as a bar room boxer; not as a shooter; not as a racegoer; nor as a drinker. He simply wanted to be known as a writer and to be judged as such.

When he was over fifty years old, Hemingway reminded a journalist that his shyness was still intact, that he felt ill at ease when he had to speak about his work, that he didn't correspond at all to the prefabricated images that are stuck on him, that he hated dinner jackets and everything they represent: "Wearing

Catholic church in Cojímar.

underwear is as formal as I ever hope to get." (A. E. Hotchner, *Papa Hemingway*.) Another writer, Norman Mailer, gives us some clues, enables us to understand a little better what lay behind all the masks that time and notoriety superimposed on a face. "Hemingway, when all is said, was a Midwestern boy seized by success and ripped out of every root, and he spent the rest of his life trying to relocate some of his old sense of terra firma by following each movement of the wind (and there were many) through his talent and his dread." (Preface to the book by Gregory H. Hemingway, *Papa*).

Hemingway hid behind his international fame, stardom, the mask of the hero incarnate, the *aficionado*, old sea dog, hunter of the African savanna. No,

Hemingway did not provoke a duel with a man who was supposed to have insulted Ava Gardner; no, he did not save Dos Passos from death on the horns of an Andalusian bull; no, he was not up to his eyes in debt when he was awarded the Nobel Prize; no, he did not free the Ritz at the head of an army of mercenaries; no, contrary to what Kurt Singer affirms, his motto was not: boats, booze, broads and books. Everyone went along with this game of flashy labels, these two–way mirrors, reflections, decoys that were nothing but so many traps. The great Alejo Carpentier himself, in one of his chronicles published in 1954, paints a portrait of Hemingway that is riddled with the kind of clichés we find in a tourist guide. Hemingway never stopped repeating that he wanted

A typical Cojímar street. The little fishing village seems not to have changed at all since *The Old man and the Sea*. "Up the road, in his shack, the old man was sleeping again. He was still sleeping on his face and the boy was sitting by him watching him. The old man was dreaming about the lions." (*The Old Man and the Sea.*)

people to analyze his work rather than his life. Hemingway was the opposite of his own legend, but he had a double to represent him, a man who, from 1933, traveled the length and breadth of the United States passing himself off as Hemingway, dedicating his books, running up debts, some of which Hemingway finally had to pay! One day he was found sailing on a junk in the China Sea, a man who nevertheless had a name: Richard Halliburton! This false Hemingway was the real one, the man of the legend. He could appear, "represent" him, but he could never have sent this letter to Charles Scribner: "Mary would not show me your letter; but she always asks me why can't I be a Gentleman like Charles Scribner instead of telling people to get that rag out of their ass and move." (*Selected Letters*, 19 July 1950).

Behind the mask was, as always, yet another mask, as Octavio Paz says. Behind fishing, another fishing: metaphysical. When Nick Adams' swamp, between the river and the trees, becomes an oily swell between the hard sun and the soft heavy clouds stationary over the Tropic of Cancer, the art of fishing appears twofold, forked, light and dark, divine essence with a diabolical principle. On the one hand, the marlin; on the other, the shark. In the first we find combat on the high seas, the primitive struggle with the trout of childhood, a noble asceticism. With the second comes hatred, theft, unhappiness. When Hemingway caught his first fish on the high seas, an enormous tuna, a shark fed on it. Bill Leeds, the millionaire, was witness to the scene. He was armed with a machine gun. Hemingway gave him no peace until he got his hands on the gun to hunt the shark with it. No holds were barred against the predator: the assault rifle, buckshot, a 22 – caliber rifle, a Thompson submachine gun – he killed 27 in two weeks. All more than 10 foot long. As soon as they showed their heads out of the water he

fired. In his "Letter from the Gulf Stream" published in Esquire in June 1953, he was formidably precise, explaining that if you ever have to shoot a shark, you should aim at any point in a straight line going right through the middle of its head from the tip of its snout to one foot behind its eyes. If you can, cut this line with a line passing between its two eyes and if you can shoot at this place, it will drop stone dead. A 22 bullet will kill it just as surely as a 45. (*By Line*). In *The Old Man and the Sea* Santiago has to fight with makoo sharks and galanos of the species called "spatula snout". They are a metaphor for fate, the ineluctable. Robert Jordan, the *Inglés* of *For Whom the Bell Tolls*, will also have them as enemies, and describes the shadows of the Heinkels sliding over the country like the shadows of sharks on a sandbank at the bottom of the ocean. And again, a few pages further on, "They are shaped like sharks, Robert Jordan thought, the wide-finned, sharp-nosed sharks of the Gulf Stream. But these, wide-finned in silver, roaring, the light mist of their propellers in the sun, these do not move like

sharks. They move like nothing there has ever been. They move like mechanized doom." Unlike Joseph Conrad's hero, who travels to the *Heart of Darkness*, Hemingway does not escape from the nightmare. The death of the shark forces him to explore his own self, to search for himself. The shark, in its violence, its blackness, forces him to return to the "Clean, Well-lighted Place" of his childhood. The Gulf Stream is the source and destination of the Big Two-Hearted River.

The adventure of the *Pilar* disguised as a spy ship is informative. It was 1940. On returning from reporting in the Far East with his young wife, Martha Gellhorn, Hemingway learnt of the death of his old fishing and drinking buddy, Joe Russell. Martha, like the journalist that she was, decided to leave for England, North Africa then Italy in order to follow the war. Hemingway preferred, for the time being, to stay in Cuba to fight his own war. He had two curious projects in mind, and successfully defended them before the Cuban government and the American ambassador Sprouille Braden, married to a Chilean woman and considered by some to be broad-minded. The first consisted of creating a counter-espionage network to gather information on Franco-ist and nazi sympathizers on the island. He nicknamed his network "The Crook Factory". The Crook Factory was active from May 1942 to April 1943 and quickly attracted the wrath of the FBI who took a dim view of an amateur treading on their terrain and did everything in their power to inveigh against the enterprise and turn it to ridicule. The second project, every bit as fantastical as the first, consisted of transforming the *Pilar* into a spy ship in charge of monitoring the operations of the Third Reich's fleet of submarines operating in the Caribbean area. Fitted out with a transmitter – receiver, a cannon, a machine gun and explosives, the *Pilar* was supposed to act as bait for possible

The café-restaurant La Terraza, in Cojímar. Frequented by Hemingway, Thomas Hudson In Islands in the Stream and, of course, by the old fisherman Santiago: "The boy had brought them in a two-decker metal container from the Terrace. The two sets of knives and forks and spoons were in his pocket with a paper napkin wrapped around each set." (*The Old Man and the Sea.*)

Gregorio Fuentes at La Terraza. Gregorio Fuentes was first mate aboard the Pilar from 1938. In the summer of 1949, he was 50 and he started sailing at Lanzarote, a little island in the canaries, at the age of 4. Hemingway met him at Dry Tortugas, when he was skipper of a fishing boat and they were both grounded in 1928 due to a strong north easterly wind.

German submarines and occasionally sink them should they venture too close to the boat! The operation was called "Friendless", after one of the cats at the *Finca*! Hemingway recruited a valiant crew: two American footballers, a millionaire polo player from Long Island, a sergeant from the embassy detachment of fusiliers and "a few local guys", Patchi, Ermua, Gregorio Fuentes. The mission lasted from June 1942 until April 1944, when Hemingway left for New York and London.

These obviously fruitless expeditions in search of submarines generally ended in drinking bouts and fights. Gregory H. Hemingway gives a savory vision of them in the chapter of his memoirs entitled "*Don Quixote vs. the Wolf Pack*". The young sailor, who was twelve years old at the time, recounts that at night they could hear the submarines conversing in German but that it was impossible to localize them because the *Pilar* did not have triangulation instruments. On one of their missions the sailors found what they thought was an enemy supply depot hidden in a cave. The passage became so tight that they sent Gregory H. ahead as a scout. His war booty was an eloquent testimony: three bottles of Schlitz beer, a German brand… produced in the United States! But we would be wrong to take this episode too lightly. The curious troupe finally tracked down German submarines that were then sunk by the American fleet. Ex–agent A-39 – or 09 – received the medal of military Valor for his services and used many of the episodes of this curious adven-

The interior of La Terraza. In *Islands in the Stream*, Thomas Hudson found his cat Boise there one sunny Christmas morning. "He remembered the frst time he had seen it when it was a kitten playing with its reflection on the glass of the tobacco counter of the Cojímar bar which was built on the rocks overlooking the port."

ture to write some of the most beautiful and despairing pages of *Islands in the Stream*, in which Thomas Hudson becomes one of Hemingway's last heroes. Besides, it is interesting to follow the characters of the novel *Islands in the Stream*, who are, for the most part, romanticized doubles of the "Friendless" operation: Henry Wood is Winston Guest, the millionaire athlete; Willie is John Saxon, the radio officer dispatched by the American embassy; Antonio is Gregorio Fuentes; Ara is Francisco Ibarlucia, the jai alai player; Juan is Juan Dunabeitia, the Basque; as for Thomas Hudson, we can imagine that he is none other than Hemingway himself. The risks they took were very real and their commitment was total. No one can doubt the sincerity of Hemingway and his crew, nor

even the reality of their experiences. Here the mask fell, as it fell in Italy in 1914, as it fell in Spain, as it later fell in the company of the soldiers of the 22nd regiment and the 4th infantry division of the 1st army. Beautiful lies and the quest for experience are two necessary qualities for the insatiable curiosity of the writer. Hemingway, although not a writer who is *engagé* or committed to a particular political cause, was certainly a writer with commitment.

Hemingway's world was a world at war. An implacable and brutal struggle for life. Rebelling against the society he was born into, rebelling against the world he lived in, Hemingway never ceased to repeat that it was possible to destroy a man but not to conquer him. Thus, his commitment, like that of the heroes of *For*

Whom the Bell Tolls, like their deaths, was solitary, but showed his solidarity. Hemingway was a man of solidarity and commitment. An attitude he acquired very young because, in April 1918, when only twenty years old, on learning that the Red Cross was seeking volunteers for the Italian army, he immediately decided to enlist. Very early on, he started to look at the world, feel it, observe it. He was very quickly in contact with violence, crimes, accidents, brutal deaths, everyday heroism, suicide. He discovered man in all his greatness and all his puniness. Martha Gellhorn, who was not yet his wife and was by his side in Spain, was won over: "It was the only time in his life, she thought, when he was not the most important thing in the world" (J. R. Mellow, *Hemingway*). It would be a safe bet to assume that this was often his attitude. There is ample proof to back up this theory. Yes, commitment is solidarity. This is the luminous meaning he gives to the quotation from John Donne that he uses as a preface to *For Whom the Bell Tolls*: "No man is an Island, self sufficient, independent; every man is a piece of the Continent, a part of the whole. If a sod be washed away by the sea, Europe is the less, as well as if a promontory were, as well as if a Manor of thy friend's or of thine own were; any man's death diminishes me, because I am a part of humanity. And therefore never ask for whom the bell tolls; it tolls for thee." It was this great humanism that made him reject the violence and gangsterism of the Batista régime and applaud the victory of Fidel Castro in 1959. The victory was that of his fishermen and peasant friends, of the Cubans to whom he owed so much.

In spite of whatever the FBI may have thought, Hemingway never described himself as a convert to Marxism but very much as a writer in a visceral struggle with all forms of fascism. He often took a stand very quickly and very early on. At a time when

Hemingway with friends at La Terraza. "They were fishermen who looked the least like fishermen he had ever known and they were among the best. They wore old straw hats or were bareheaded. They wore old clothes and were sometimes barefoot or sometimes wore shoes." (*Islands in the Stream.*)

Advertisement for Hatuey beer, very popular aboard the *Pilar*.

Club de Cazadores del Cerro. 'I'm shooting over 94% on pigeons and this is always a good sign of how things are going,' Hemingway wrote to his eldest son, on October 16, 1949. (*Selected Letters*.)

Situated in the district of Cerro, the Club de Cazadores was frequented by the Creole aristocracy, the intellectual bourgoisie and rich Americans close to those in power. All kinds of shooting were practiced there, including clay and live pigeons.

many American correspondents in Italy were applauding Mussolini's accession to power, he was one of the rare ones to describe him as a pathetic character and the greatest bluffer in Europe. He reacted vigorously to the assassination of the socialist deputy, Matteotti.

"Half a million dead wops
And he got a kick out of it
The son of a bitch."

He wrote in a poem that took D'Annunzio as a target. (88 poems) He didn't hesitate to lend a helping hand to the opposition plotting against the dictator Trujillo. He broke off with Ezra Pound when the latter expressed anti-Semitic and fascist ideas. The speech he made in June 1937 in the course of a congress of American writers at the Carnegie Foundation in New York could not have been more explicit, treating Fascism as a lie, and saying that a writer who did not want to lie could neither write nor live under fascism. The writer of commitment opposed the arbitrary.

Although it may initially seem that Hemingway took a subjective and sentimental stance in the great historical battle of men, it is evident that over the years his attitude became more realistic, more concrete. Nick Adams was struggling against evil; Hemingway fought against its terrestrial manifestations. In the summer of 1937, recounts his brother Leicester, he

dispensed treasures of eloquence on his friends and acquaintances to persuade them to come to the help of the Spanish Republic. (*Hemingway, My Brother*). Like Martha, Hemingway thought that the writer had been put on earth to accomplish a mission, that talent was not enough if not combined with a conscience. What does Hemingway tell us? That the problem the writer has to face is immutable, whatever its origin. That it is always a question, when it comes right down to it, of discovering the truth. Tracking it, like a detective, cornering it and reconstituting it for the reader so that he can make it his own. The writer's duty is to make a gift of his truth to the reader. It was fashionable in the thirties to preach a "socially responsible" literature and

Hemingway began to frequent the Club de Cazadores del Cerro at the beginning of the forties. He and his younger son won many pigeon shooting competitions here.

to consider a book like *Death in the Afternoon* as frivolous or even reactionary. How wrong that would be! Hemingway was never uncommitted, but he was determined to keep his distance from all dogma and all systems. I remember an old Yugoslav writer, Dusan Matíc, the father of Serbo-Croat surrealism, telling me about the "terrible jaws of dialectics" and the necessity for the writer to take a step back from all systems. Hemingway, in more or less the same words, makes the same point, when he wrote that when a man can and wants to write, no critical system can damage his work if it is good, nor save it if it is bad. (*By Line*). Hemingway is never indifferent, in terms of social or literary values. He amply showed his solidarity with the human race.

It was this love of the human race, of his fellow being, that earned him the wrath of the FBI, who built up a 113-page file against him, as it did for 135 other American writers, among them James Baldwin, Erskine Caldwell, John Dos Passos, William Faulkner, F. Scott Fitzgerald, Dashiell Hammett, Sinclair Lewis, Carson Mc Cullers, Norman Mailer, Arthur Miller, Anaïs Nin, Ezra Pound, John Reed, Upton Sinclair, Gertrude Stein, John Steinbeck, Edith Wharton and William Carlos Williams. What did they have against him? As early as 1935 he was described as "a special writer." He was accused of having bought two ambulances for republican Spain. Under close surveillance in Cuba, he was not overly perturbed, due to the friendship between Martha Gellhorn and Eleanor

"The live pigeon shooting is the most exciting," Gregory Hemingway wrote, in *Hemingway, Papa*. "Don't worry about hitting the pigeons, Gig, just concentrate on your form," Papa would tell me. "If you fire enough shots you'll start to get the leads down, that is, you'll learn hox far to fire in front of a bird flying at an angle to you. The shot doesn't get there as soon as the gun goes off, you know."

Roosevelt. In 1949 the FBI again took an interest in the "Hemingway case". In 1954 his involvement with Ava Gardner and Frank Sinatra, known to have Mafia connections, earned him further attention. In 1959 it was obviously brought to the attention of the FBI that Hemingway had kissed the Cuban flag and made statements that were considered to be anti-American. The FBI found it strange that Hemingway should be hospitalized in Rochester under a false name! Lastly, two years before his death, they were worried that Cuba might issue a stamp bearing an effigy of Ernest Hemingway and thus lead the general public to believe that "Hemingway was a confident of Fidel Castro and conclude that they were fellow travelers or

something of the sort" (Natalie Robins, *Le FBI et les écrivains*, Albin Michel). In fact, the FBI was not spying on Hemingway through fear that he might establish links with communists but essentially because he overtly criticized the directors of the Bureau. Had he not declared in the middle of the war, when he had transformed the *Pilar* into a floating arsenal, that the FBI was a "dangerous" organization, going so far as to compare it with the Gestapo? All this would have been quite amusing if the consequences in terms of Hemingway's mental health had not been so dramatic. Without going so far as to hold the FBI responsible for Hemingway's death, it is worth bearing in mind that he knew he was under observation, being followed, and his telephone tapped. Before his death he was convinced that the FBI had made a target of him and was spying on him. On Saturday July 1, 1961, the day before his death, while dining in a restaurant with Mary and a friend, he noticed two individuals at a table. They reassured him that the men were salesmen. Hemingway was convinced they were FBI agents. In her book, Natalie Robins quotes an ominous phrase from Arthur Miller, to the effect that the FBI's capacity to terrify people was immense. Today we know that Hemingway's phone was bugged and that some of his letters were intercepted. At the time, nobody wanted to believe him. His son, Gregory H. wrote: "His first noticeable symptoms of paranoia began, with the worry about the FBI chasing him for income tax evasion." His old friend A. E. Hotchner invokes one of his last visits to Ketchum and shows a depressed Hemingway obsessed with the "feds", going so far as to envisage that he, A. E. Hotchner, was perhaps part of the conspiracy mounted against him. It is difficult not to remember Arthur Miller's sentence. What is the price of commitment? What price do we have to pay to be true to our convictions? These ques-

Since 1961, the double-barelled Remingtons of the Club de Cazadores del Cerro are no longer fired at pigeons, but have been replaced by the submachine guns of the Revolutionary Miltary Academy.

In a letter to Hadley Mowrer, July 23, 1942, Hemingway wrote that he would hate to die, for every year he enjoyed fishing and hunting more. He added that he enjoyed fishing and hunting as much as he did when he was sixteen.

Hemingway started boxing while studying at Oak Park High School. In the book which he wrote on Hemingway, Robert Escarpit remarked that Hemingway had always been impressed by boxing and its false violence. The character of the boxer who "takes" punches as a job had always fascinated him.

tions are still valid today.

All literary commitment demands its share of solitude. And in this share, and in this solitude, dissatisfaction, worry, clear-sightedness, despair. Herbert Matthews rightly considers that Hemingway knew "how to be a man at the critical moments". Hemingway, as he once advised his old friend Marlene Dietrich on an evening when he was feeling low, never confuse "motion with action". A very literary commitment, the commitment of life to death.

Hemingway is neither a "committed" nor a "non-committed" writer. His commitment is on another level, somewhere between the African safaris and the waters of the Gulf Stream, between Nick Adams' childhood and the wanderings of Thomas Hudson. Hemingway's commitment is that of a life: the commitment to surpass the self. And more than that, a new form of generosity. Basically, what Jordan says in *For Whom the Bell Tolls* is that the world is beautiful; the world is worth fighting for, worth dying for. Yes, Hemingway was magnanimous, and didn't keep accounts in friendship. He gave of himself, and even squandered, in the face of arrogance of all sorts, irony,

cynicism, and even worse, condescension. Faced with failure after the publication of *Across the River and Into the Trees*. The English writer Evelyn Waugh who was not usually so gentile, found the right formula: "Why do they all hate Hemingway so much? I believe they recognized something quite unforgivable in his work: a moral. Behind all the boasting, the anathema, the fisticuffs, an elementary chivalry comes to light: respect for women, pity for the weak, a sense of honor." (A. E. Hotchner, *Hemingway and His World*). Commitment is ethical.

This is the way life should be. Santiago communes with his fish – "All that makes me sad, fish. It destroys everything we have done," (*The Old Man and the Sea*) – like David and Andrew in *Islands in the Stream*. Men

and fish confused. David hooks an enormous fish, bigger than a marlin, more enormous than a swordfish, and then loses it, line broken. "If you'd have had caught him," Andrew said, "you'd have been probably the most famous young boy in the world." […] "What about the fish? Wouldn't he be famous?" David asked. […] "He'd be most famous of all," Andrew said, "he'd be immortal."

So David confides:

"Well," David said with his eyes tight shut. "In the worst parts, when I was the tiredest I couldn't tell which was him and which was me."

"I understand," Roger said.

"Then I began to love him more than anything on earth." […]

"Now I don't give a shit I lost him," David said. "I don't care about records. I just thought I did. I'm glad that he's all right and that I'm all right. We aren't enemies."

The man and the fish are brothers. When the old man struggles he doesn't think about death. His combat with the sharks is that of the cruelty that assails human existence. He struggles for an unhoped for victory, telling himself that by holding on until the end, he will hold on eternally. Resisting is acting. Being is a state of becoming.

Bergson advised his students to act as men of thought and to think as men of action. Hemingway streamlined the principle and only kept the essence: for his heroes, thinking is unthinkable. Thus the old man is not struggling with death, but with life. Santiago is not Harry who looks death in the face in profound solitude. The effort, the meaning of life, a solitary existence, everything is pushed to the limit in *The Old Man and the Sea*. But this book is never a symbol for the absolute. However we look at it, the old man breaks a record. A ridiculous record, but one

Hemingway adored what Norberto Fuentes described as the "bloody beauty of cock fights". He raised fighting cocks at *Finca Vigía*. His son, Gregory, wrote that he remembered being upset at the typically Havanese spectacle because of "the greed of the gamblers".

that tells us a lot about the meaning Hemingway wanted to give to this episode: by letting Santiago return empty-handed ninety four days in succession, he made him beat the record set by Zane Grey, who only stayed ninety three days without bringing anything back to port! Man is therefore his own measure and his only yardstick. It doesn't have to be a matter of death for him. The man can die in imperceptible whisperings, like in *The Snows of Kilimanjaro*, or very quickly, like Paco in *Death in the Afternoon*, a bullfighter's death, the femoral artery severed, without even having the time to lose his illusions. We must remember: death is not Santiago's goal, nor is it Hemingway's focal point. Hemingway never tired of repeating that the sea was the sea. The old man was an

The Vedado Tennis Club, at 12 y Calzada, in the Vedado. Hemingway was a member of one of the most exclusive clubs in Havana, mentioned in the best Guides of the 1920's along side clubs such as the Centro Asturiano, and the Centro Gallego, the Club Automovil de Cuba and the Club Femenino de Cuba.

The Fronton Habana-Madrid. The matches were the subject of legal betting. The advert states that the Fronton was also a casino.

old man. The young boy was a young boy and the fish was a fish. The sharks were all sharks, no better nor worse. (J. R. Mellow, *Hemingway*). Santiago is a fisherman who loves the sea and lives by it. No symbolism, no Franciscan mysticism, no ritual. This is literature that is precise and naked. Modern literature become classical. Direct literature, with no obliqueness, prevarication or traps. *The Old Man and the Sea* is a simple story: that of an old man who catches a fish. Fishing and writing are part of the same nature. The fisherman, like the writer, could apply the words of Doctor Rieux in *The Plague*: "The main thing is to do one's job well". Work accomplished; this is the yardstick by which we measure a man. No legendary resonances, no mystical quests, no confessions. The destination is of little importance. Only the journey counts. The movement of a caravan in the desert, changing place, the exertion of effort. Things may have been hopeless, but Hemingway could not resign himself to not changing them. It is only after this, after these leaps into the void, that death can come into play.

Homer made death the only really serious question, Hemingway adds writing. Pain, also, when it refuses consolation. Far removed from metaphysics, death, like life, like writing, is a simple matter – like fishing. The famous old double dicho, on which *The Old Man and the Sea* is based – "man can be destroyed, but not defeated; man can be defeated, but not destroyed" – cannot be overcome except by death. Only death can defeat man. Death, a major theme in Hemingway's work, the subject of half of his short stories, the main theme of seven of his novels! Where does the preoccupation with death come from? From childhood; always from childhood. The suicide of his father, who shot himself through the base of his skull on December 6th 1928, was to haunt him to the end of his days. All his life Hemingway felt the breath of the Reaper with the scythe. Sometimes in strange ways, like the airplane accident when he was flying over northwestern Uganda, and which earned him very some premature obituary notices.

In *For Whom the Bell Tolls*, Robert Jordan helps himself to die, i.e. he refuses the temptation to kill himself in order to avoid doing the same thing as his father. One day Hemingway confided to Robert Manning that he saw suicide as the last resort of an egotist, indifferent to his own entourage. What happened? On June 15, 1961 he wrote one of his last letters to the son of doctor Savier, Fritz, then aged nine and hospitalized for a viral heart ailment. It ended with a statement that he felt very good and very optimistic in general, and that hoped to see them all soon. Seventeen days later, on July 2 1961, he blew off his skull with a double-barreled shotgun. He died at Ketchum and not in Cuba: "Going away can be final. Walking out the door can be final. Any form of real betrayal can be final. Dishonesty can be final. Selling out is final. But you are just talking now. Death is what is really final." (*Islands in the Stream*).

Having been left for a long time in a corner of Havana harbor, the wreck of the *Pilar*, stripped of its Universal and Chrysler engines and fishing equip-

The hall of the Fronton Habana-Madrid, frequented by Hemingway. They played jai alai – pronounced "High-Ally" – there, according to the American tourist guides of the time. Seats were $2 each, or you could rent a box for six people. The famous General Guide Havana, written for American tourists, specified that "Children of both sexes can watch the matches." "...they call the place where they play Basque pelot the Horno Verde or the Green Oven because it is painted green inside and gets so hot." (*Selected Letters.*)

FOLLOWING DOUBLE PAGE: Hemingway told Robert Manning (Atlantic Monthly, August 1965) that the ocean was our last place of liberty.

ment, finally landed at the *Finca Vigía*. For a while Mary had wanted to have the *Pilar* towed out to the high seas and scuttled off Cojímar. The Cuban authorities were opposed to this project and preferred to transfer the rusted carcass of the old boat to the middle of the palm trees and bougainvillea at San Francisco de Paula. What a strange sight to see this boat, half-décor, half mausoleum! A boat on dry land, surrounded by rustling bamboo, a few feet away from an empty swimming pool and the graves of four of Hemingway's dogs: Nero, Negrita, Linda and Black Dog. A boat never batted by the sea. Death, Hemingway liked to repeat, "is just one more whore"! We can bet that Hemingway's death did not encounter Hemingway's god, this strange god that ignores transcendence, who only exists for man as a malaise or a fear, a crack or an incomplete destiny. In his life, in his work, Hemingway did nothing but trace the line that separates Nick Adams from Santiago. Michel del Castillo was right, "it is neither character nor age, it is experience" that separates the primitive adolescent

The first Ernest-Hemingway fishing competition. It took place on May 27, 1950. In the foreground, the Avenida C. Manuel de Céspedes, with the Bay of Havana and the Morro lighthouse.

Water Front M.Ylla.-May-27-50.

from the old fisherman. It took the writer a whole lifetime to transform his defeat into a victory, therefore into freedom. Hemingway, like Goethe, knew that we were born alone and die alone. He joins the other great observers of this deplorable human event that is death: Hamlet, Kierkegaard, Unamuno, Saint John of the Cross, Pascal, Emmanuel Kant in his last days. After the death of the Indian, the child Nick asks if it is hard to die. Hemingway's greatness was not that he answered that question, but that he understood that it was not a subject for literature. We must live the question of death before responding to it. The Hemingway hero was Hemingway himself, with his taste for the final failure of life. A failure, Santiago tells us that is accepted, borne, lived. A failure that is not transformed into fate, philosophy, asceticism. A failure that is nothing more than a way of being, of expressing oneself. One day, a fisherman who was intrigued by the strange criticism in a Havana newspaper that insisted on the "symbolic" side of *The Old Man and the Sea*, asked Hemingway what symbolism was? "*Symbolismo, es un truco nuevo de los intellectuales*" answered the writer. Hemingway's work is unmediated, straight, rectilinear, with no cross-currents. Making its way in the great river, the mountain river, the Gulf Stream, the torrent and current out of Ecclesiastes: "One generation passeth away, and another generation cometh: but the earth abideth for ever. The sun also riseth and the sun goeth down."

What more can be said, looking at the *Pilar* moored in a phantom property peopled with all the pasts of the island, *santería* and Spain, Africa, cats and dogs, rifles and marlins, children, alcohol? The bull is neurotic in the arena and healthy in the field. That's all, said Hemingway. Put a man in the field. Put a man in the arena. Take a child out of the primitive nature of Lake Walloon and throw him into "this dirty world".

At the time, the Sailing Club was in competition with the Polo Club and the Yacht Club.

Hemingway described life as "grace under pressure". A whole way of seeing things… And what if he were one of those who spoke best of love? André Malraux said this was so and compared him to Stendhal. Hemingway's boat can become as light as Santiago's. When he has neither feelings nor thoughts. When he is thinking of nothing except bringing his writing into port as well and as intelligently as possible… I read somewhere that "far from the stimulating presence of intellectual equals, Hemingway had become closer to a screen idol than to a writer." The opposite is true! The literary catch that Hemingway painstakingly landed was experience, a grappling with nature, that one-to-one relationship with the world that is the writer's very existence, that is existence *tout court*. Nature was

his sounding-board, his intellectual stimulation, his inspiration and raw material. Not what other people thought of the world but first-hand experience of that world. This was what he tried to portray and communicate to the reader, in such a way that the reader could then draw their own conclusions from an experience so skillfully crafted as to create the impression of having been shared. At the opposite end of the literary scale from introspective writers in love with language per se, from the flourishes of romanticism, Hemingway at his best makes language disappear in favor of the existential being that exists outside language. It has often been said that art is an attempt to provide an adequate response to nature, and Hemingway's work is surely one of the most success-

The Cuban edition of *The Old Man and the Sea*. Published in the form of a special edition of Life, on September 1, 1952, *The Old Man and the Sea* was published a week later by Scribner. Hemingway was awarded the Pulitzer prize for literature for this book, in May 1953.

RIGHT HAND PAGE: The International Fishing Club, in the Port of Havana. Hemingway wrote, in "A Letter from Cuba", published in Esquire in 1933, that the main reason for living in Cuba was the big deep blue river, a mile deep and sixty to eighty miles wide.

ful attempts to do just that – by taking up the most formidable physical challenges, to win the battle with that 'eternity or the lack of it' he mentioned in his Nobel Prize acceptance speech. "Write about what you know", he would say, and Hemingway did not miss a detail of his surroundings, was himself intimately involved in the deeds and actions, the experiences of his fellow creatures, great and small. His hikes in the Cuban countryside and his excursions on the *Pilar* reminded him of the lakes and forests of upper Michigan. Not in the company of intellectuals, but with sharks and marlins, birds and swordfish, drunkards, fishermen and peasants. Hemingway carried inside himself a whole world of rage and delicacy, insolence, languor and tenderness. As a clear-sighted writer he was struggling with himself: to write or not to write. Or how to continue to write? How to keep one's freedom, even if one has to kill oneself to do so? How to continue learning to observe for ever? How to

be present? How to live with this death that is of no importance except that it kills those we love? I would like to end with a letter that Ernest Hemingway sent from a holiday camp to his mother in August 1914. He was fifteen years old: "Dear Mom – I got your card, thank you very much. Our train was 2 hours and 25 minutes late! so no school. The programme has been turned upside down, lunch at a different time and a pile of other changes. The rumor went around that I was drowned and some of my pals thought I was a ghost. CAN I PLEASE HAVE LONG TROUSERS. All the other boys in our class have them, Lewis Clarahan, Ignatz Smith and all the other little runts. My trousers are so tight that every time I move I think they are going to split and I have about eight or ten inches under my cuffs. Please say I can have long ones. Your drowned son Ernest Hemingway. RSVP Quickly. P.S. My shirt buttons all burst when I breathe deeply." (*Selected Letters*).

HEMINGWAY:
Guía General

I still believe that the writer has nothing to gain by providing keys to his work. He writes to be read. All commentary, all explanation seem superfluous to me.

Ernest Hemingway, in Paris Review, Spring 1958.

AUTOMOBILES

There have been beautiful American cars. And now, according to some, there will therefore be beautiful Cuban cars. Many of them are nothing but the shadow of what they used to be. Ostentatious and ramshackle phantoms emerging from the fifties, in the same way as the old Mack trucks, a testimony to the American capitalism of pre-Revolution era. After 1961 it was forbidden to import the Cadillacs, Oldsmobiles, Chevrolets, Packards, Studebakers and other shining monsters which were, in Hemingway's day, commonplace on the narrow streets of La Habana Vieja or on the broad avenues of Vedado or Miramar. Latin American literature has often paid homage to these vehicles that Batista did not disdain to use, nor did Castro and Che Guevara. We only have to think of the nostalgic pages devoted to them by Guillermo Cabrera Infante in *Three Sad Tigers* when he evokes the euphoria of a certain promenade "aboard a convertible on the Malecon between five and

Hemingway owned a Buick Station Wagon, a Chrysler pick-up and a 1955 Chrysler convertible.

The neocolonial patio of the Museum of Numismatology. Calle Oficios, 8. A stone's throw from the Hotel Ambos Mundos.

seven o'clock on August 11th 1958, at a hundred, a hundred and twenty, with the summer sun turning red on an indigo sea, in the middle of clouds that sometimes dropped everything and made a twilight like the end of a Technicolor religious film". But also Juan, the hero of *Cuban Rhapsody* by Eduardo Manet, who leaves Havana seated on the back seat of his father Edelmiro Sargats' "gleaming Cadillac Continental, at cruising speed while the day was dawning". Tourist guidebooks between the thirties and the fifties remind us that the roads are safe, giving the distances separating Havana and the main cities and the list of dealers for the big automobile brands. As early as 1923 Ford set up a car rental system with drivers, similar to the taxi system. It cost 3 dollars for four people to go from the city center to the Colón cemetery. Facing Central Park and opposite the Inglaterra and Telégrafo hotels luxurious cars were made available to tourists without a chauffeur. Hemingway did not need to have recourse to these zealous services. He had a Buick Station Wagon, a Chrysler pick-up and a 1955 Chrysler convertible "painted fire-engine red", bought new for $3924 and which Juan, the chauffeur, took out on grand occasions. Juan Pastor recounts that Ernest sometimes vomited between the Floridita and the *Finca* or peed on the seats of the Buick, claiming it was the tiger from the Ringling circus that had done it! One June evening in 1945, after a drinking session, Hemingway took the wheel, his car rolled over, his head hit the rear-view mirror and he injured his knee. In October 1953, on the Carretera Central, he went into the ditch, cut his face and sprained his shoulder…

The beautiful old Cuban cars that are still roadworthy are "unofficial" taxis, less expensive and less reliable than the Intur taxis. The street is their real museum, although there is

quite a disappointing museum only a couple of steps away from the Ambos Mundos hotel and the Numismatic Museum in which we can discover, in the shade of a magnificent colonial patio, two old specimens of Bolita, the Cuban game of chance that made the underworld rich…

• The Museum of Old Cars.
Oficios, 13 (between Obispo and Lamparilla).

BARS

Cafés de Paris (Obispo and San Ignacio), with its old fans; **Mirador**, behind **La Divina Pastora**, overlooking Havana Bay; the **bar of the Inglaterra** hotel (Prado, between Rafael and Neptuno); **Aire Mar** and **Sirena**, in the Nacional hotel (21st street and O street.-Vedado); the Andalusian **patio of the Sevilla** hotel (Trocadero, 55), a few steps away from the **house of Lezama Lima** (Trocadero, 162) transformed into a museum. They are born and die in accordance with economic ups and downs or live on in certain historical sites. Hemingway frequented many of them. **La Casa Recalt** (Obispo, between Ignacio and Cuba) and **Sloppy Joe's** (252, Zulueta-Agramonte, between Trocadero and Animas) are now nothing more than decrepit facades from which we can only vaguely guess at their former splendor. His two favorite bars – **la Bodeguita del medio** and the **Floridita** – have become Hemingway shrines. The first, wrongly so, the second, rightly. La Bodeguita del medio, founded by Ángel Martínez, was originally a grocery – la Casa Martínez – where one could find, next to drinks, lard and beans, eggs and spices and all sorts of other fare. When Félix Ayón, the publisher-printer, set up shop in Empedrado street in about 1946 he developed the habit of coming to the house of Ángel Martínez to make phone calls and made appointments with his correspondents "at the bodega in the middle of the street, exactly in the middle". Little by little the grocery-café came to be respected as a place where one could even eat. The manager employed Silvia Torres, who replaced Madam Martínez at the stoves and introduced typically Cuban food: chilindrón, picadillo, moros y cristianos, tasajo… What the Americans call Creole food. On April 26, 1950, according to legend, the Casa Martínez was renamed la Bodeguita del Medio. Now frequented by Nicolás Guillén and Alejo Carpentier, Beny Moré and Wilfredo Lam, Julio Cortázar and Gabriel García Márquez, Mariano and

• **El Floridita**, Montserrate, n° 557 (corner of Obispo).
• **La Bodeguita del medio**, Empedrado, n° 207
(between Cuba and San Ignacio). Bar and restaurant.
• **Bibliography**: *El Floridita*, Fernando G. Campoamor.
Editorial Científico-Técnica, Ciudad de La Habana, 1993.
La Bodeguita del medio, Rafael Lam. Inst. cubano del libro, 1994.

ABOVE: The statuette from the Floridita.

BELOW: Cerro Stadium "He thought of the Big Leagues, to him they were the Gran Ligas, and he knew that the Yankees of New York were playing the Tigers of Detroit." (*The Old Man and the Sea.*)

Portocarrero, it quickly became a fashionable and trendy place in the Cuba of the nineteen fifties. Errol Flynn, Nat King Cole, Jimmy Durante and Lou Costello had taken up the habit of frequenting it, not to mention Martine Carol and Brigitte Bardot. It is easy to understand that Hemingway did not go there willingly, although the Bodeguita was the home of the refreshing mojito. The sentence on the wall of the establishment, attributed to Hemingway – "My mojito at the Bodeguita, my daiquiri at the Floridita" – is of course apocryphal…

The Floridita is genuinely a Hemingway haunt. Established just behind the old Monserrate gates closing the ramparts of La Habana Vieja, La Pina de Plata was originally a bar where vermouth, gin and cognac but also Draque, the ancestor of the cocktail, were served. Industrial manufacture of ice in the United States at the end of the nineteenth century, and the mass influx of barmen rendered unemployed by Prohibition were behind the development of the Floridita. On returning from the First World War the Catalan Constantino Ribalaigua Vert "barman not just bartender" took over the management of the bar-restaurant, appointed a French chef, started a veritable school for barmen and added ice to the daiquiri, the alcoholic mixture invented by a mining engineer working in a remote area of the East… Constantino invented 150 cocktails, including the "Hemingway special", still known as "Papa's special".

Hemingway discovered the Floridita in 1932 and made it his haunt from 1939 onward, the date when he set up at the *Finca*. "Every time I enter this establishment, I am sure of finding fellow countrymen. In a certain sense, I'm happier to be American here than if I lived in New York." (Reported by Robert Manning, Atlantic Monthly, August 1965.)

BÉISBOL

Introduced to Cuba at the end of the nineteenth century – and not, as some think, derived from the ancient "batey" of the Taino Indians – while the American influence was progressively replacing the Spanish predominance, baseball is the most popular sport on the island. Travel throughout Cuba, there isn't one provincial capital, one factory, one production unit, one university or one village that doesn't have its own team. As in the streets of New York, squares and vacant lots are taken over by kids who organize improvised baseball matches. Although forbidden in certain parts of the island in 1895 by the Spanish authorities who saw a link between it and the independentist claims of José Marti's movement, it is true that today the sport has excellent results with the national team both Olympic Champion and World Champion!

The fifties indisputably marked the high point of base-

ball in Cuba. It was not unusual at the time to find North American players coming to swell Cuban teams between two seasons, attracted both by the mildness of the climate and the impressive salaries. Similarly, many Cuban players left for the United States and returned for tournaments on their native soil. Rich, steeped in adulation, driving Cadillacs, suitcases full of gifts, they seized the opportunity to star in small local teams and become little league players again.

The baseball player was – and still is – an idol. Santiago, in *The Old Man and the Sea*, confirms this. His interest in the private life of the great John J. McGraw, "who often came to La Terraza in the past", as the boy comments, or in the private lives of other baseball stars like Joe Di Maggio, Dick Sisler and some Cuban Managers like Adolfo Luque or Mike González, is typically Cuban: "The great Di Maggio, would he hold onto a fish as long as I do? he wondered. No mistake about it. Longer even, he would hang on even longer because he's strong. And we mustn't forget that his father was a fisherman…"

• **Cerro baseball stadium**
(with a metal frame covering since the 50s).

CABARETS

In one of his "Chronicles" published in Carteles in 1932, Alejo Carpentier reports that a particularly austere private detective was worried that the rumba as danced in salons might lead the dancers to preoccupations "of a strictly erotic order". To which comment a certain Harry Pilcer replied: "What a strange idea of dancing! How sad to forget the blues, the off-beat rhythms of the *son*, to give oneself up to lasciviousness. Let it be quite clear that the individuals who are capable of exhibiting such behavior – in a dancing hall are the very same ones that the police would be forced to arrest for having committed acts "that offend public morality!" in the street outside theatres and cinemas.

Dancing is like a religion for Cubans. Whether it be the *danzón* – a quadrille brought to the country by French buccaneers, the *son*, which derives from it (enriched with African percussion), its cousins the rumba, the *comparsa* and *guaracha*; the *mambo* in the thirties, the cha-cha-cha in the fifties, influenced by jazz from Louisiana, dancing is an integral part of Cuban culture. No trace of this fascination can be detected either in Hemingway's work or in the record col-

lection at the *Finca Vigía*. However, here again, from 1939 to 1959 there was an unprecedented spread of radio, television and cabarets in Havana. The bourgeoisie, whether *grande* or *petite*, flocked to the concerts given by Rita Montaner, Rosita Fornés, Bebo Valdés or Orestes Lopez, who filled the halls: "The spread of international tourism, the influx of North Americans, the cabarets of Havana and Varadero where they came to get drunk on rhythm and exoticism, all this was to constitute a trampoline that would send groups of Cuban boys all over the world. Anglicism and Hispanism co-existed very well at the time," writes Joseph Grelier in *Cuba, Carrefour des Caraïbes*.

Besides the Marianao Casino, with a dance band that was known to be the best in Cuba and the Cabaret Montmartre, offering a high-class show, many other places presented dance shows or organized dance evenings: The Havana Country Club, the Sans-Souci, The Pirates' Club out off the sands of Cojimar-Beach, the Clerk Club and the Centro Gallego Club. But the most famous of all, opened in 1931 and with its own casino, is still the Tropicana, situated in the Marianao district. "The most luxurious Cabaret in the world, in which the winter cold very quickly melted in the spicy heat of its gold and silver curtain" (Guillermo Cabrera Infante). It is still active and well worth a visit. On its open-air main floor surrounded by giant tropical trees swirling with catwalks and stairs, two hundred dancers put on a kitsch and atrociously unforgettable spectacle, dripping with lamé, fake jewelery, fake furs, feathers and glitter. As advertising from the fifties affirms: "Paradise beneath the stars", with the ghosts of Nat King Cole, Carmen Miranda, Beny Moré and Perez Prado looking on…

• **Tropicana.**
Calle 72, between the 43rd street and Linea Marianao.
• **El S·bado de la Rumba.**
3rd and 4th Avenida, Vedado (every two weeks).
• **Salon Copa.**
Hotel Riviera, Avenida Paseo and Malecón, Vedado.
• **Café Cantante.**
Paseo y 39, Vedado.
• But nothing can beat a **pena**, an improvised party with dancing and drinking with friends.

Advertisement for Tropicana, 1950. "The cabaret could, it's true, be presented as fabulous externally, but the show comprises half-naked women dancing the rumba and singers shouting their stupid songs and in the style of the old Bing Crosby, but singing in Spanish." (Guillermo Cabrera Infante, *Trois tristes tigres*, Gallimard.)

CAYOS

In *Cuba, Socialisme et développement*, René Dumont reminds us that Cubans don't like us to say "the island of Cuba", especially because Cuba's ownership of the second largest island, Dos Pinos, was long contested by the United States, and also because there is a multitude of islets, the *cayos* – from the English 'key'. Scattered all around the Grande Terre, these 1,600 isles and islets make up the Cuban archipelago and cover an area of 1,434 square miles. Mostly uninhabited, these tiny islands of white sand and rocks, where palm trees and red mangroves grow, are preserved realms where all the animals of the Caribbean live in total freedom: pink flamingoes, herons, cormorants, different types of hummingbird, pelicans, ospreys, turtles, iguanas, caimans and crocodiles. Before drowning himself in the Caribbean sea on April 27,

1932 the American poet Hart Crane sang of the links between the Florida keys and the Cuban cayos in a collection he was preparing to send to his publisher: *Key West: An Island Sheaf*. For more than thirty years Hemingway never ceased to criss-cross these fragments of a continent contained in a warm turquoise-blue sea. He fished there, liked to swim there completely naked and sometimes he worked there. *Islands in the Stream, To Have and Have Not, The Old Man and the Sea*, and many of his Chronicles, written between 1933 and 1956, make reference to the cayos in the Sabana-Camagüey archipelago (east of Cuba) as well as the Nuevitas, but most of all to the Megano de Casigua, three hundred kilometers to the west of Havana. He had given it the nickname Cayo Paraíso. In a letter to Mary from the front, dated November 18, 1944, he wrote: "We row and then we dock and our legs brush against each other and we drink a large glass of coconut milk, lemon and gin, and we look at the beautiful blue miniature mountains over our right shoulder and I say to you: 'Pickle, do you love me?' And then the night falls and the next day is a different day and in the morning we sleep until whatever time we like and we take our breakfast and then we throw ourselves into the water and we swim to the shore and we walk on the beach in the distance, naked." A drawing by Hemingway sent to Mary Welsh for her birthday shows Cayo Paraíso surrounded by depth measurements and renamed Treasure Island... Many of these cayos are now accessible to tourists by air and by sea.

- **Cayo largo**, in the Canarreos archipelago, between Cayo Avalo and Cayo de Díos.
- **Cayo Guillermo**, in the Camag‚ey archipelago, off the province of Ciego de Avila.
- **Cayo Coco**, to the west of Cayo Guillermo.

CIGARS

Tobacco is a legend, a vast mythology. It is the source of dreams. It crosses history. Is it not said that José Martí sent the written order marking the start of the insurrection against the Spanish occupier rolled up in a cigar? For the Taino Indians *tabaco* meant both the plant (the dried leaves) and the cigar. On landing at Cuba Christopher Columbus noticed that the Indios "never went anywhere without a brand in their fingers or without the herbs whose aroma they

Couple dancing on the patio of the Hotel Sevilla. "Dance is rhythm, the harmonious movement of muscles. How sad it is in front of a dance band to not let yourself be carried away by the pure pleasure of such a graceful movement." (Alejo Carpentier, *Chroniques*, Gallimard)

"Deep brown, with no spots, supple and firm to the touch, never breaking, strong without bitterness, a havana cigar burns smoothly and the ash does not fall. That ash! All cigar smokers know that it must make even circles and only fall off when tapped by the finger. In the presence of a true amateur, it would be considered bad taste to use a cigar cutter and even worse to stick a match in the end you are going to put to your lips: the cigar should be bitten, and the end is taken off discreetly with the teeth. And don't forget to take the ring off before you light it." (Jean Grelier, *Cuba carrefour des Caraïbes*, Société continentale d'éditions modernes illustrées.)

habitually inhaled". The rest is history. Tobacco was cultivated at Toledo as early as the sixteenth century in gardens where cicadas sang, called cigarras in Castillian and which became "cigares". Then came sailors who feared Havana-colored skies, harbingers of storms and bad weather, and created the nice expression "coup de tabac" to describe a sudden storm at sea... Next came Jean Nicot and Sir Walter Raleigh, etc. Ever since Seville – the world's first cigar capital in 1717, thanks to the imperialist *estanco de tabaco* – made Cuba the exclusive producer for the Spanish Crown, Pinar del Río tobacco has been the finest in the world.

Unlike cigarettes, cigar production is not mechanized:

a Grand Havana – a name given a trifle abusively to all cigars made from Cuban tobacco – is always hand rolled. The motions never change. The cigar maker takes the leaf from the damp cloth where it lies, stretches it on his cabinet-maker's bench, cuts the sides with the *chaveta*, delicately rolls the filler tobacco, makes the bunch, dresses the head and foot then glues the wrapper with a special rice-based glue; finally, he cuts the ends. It takes him two minutes to make a *tabaco*. Cuba produces 60 million of them every year.

There are five sorts of tobacco in Cuba: Oriente (Ciego de Ávila), Remedios (Villa Clara, Sancti Spiritus), Semi Vuelta and Vuelta Abajo (Pinar del Río), Partido (the province of Havana). Suave or strong, the most famous cigars have names like: Cohiba, Romeo y Julieta, Partagas, Hoyo de Monterrey, Bolívar, La Corona, Upmann, Monte Christo.

And let's not forget that Castro no longer smokes his famous chair legs (his doctors have forbidden them), and that Hemingway never touched a cigar in his life because he was afraid the smoke might diminish his hunter's sense of smell.

• **Casa Partagás.**
Calle Industria, no. 524.
• **Corona.**
Calle Zulueta (Agramonte), n°. 106, between El Refugio and Colón.
• **La Casa del Habano.**
Avenidas 5 and 6, Miramar.

La Terraza, in Cojímar.

Gregorio Fuentes,
quarter master on the *Pilar*.

COJÍMAR

Twenty five kilometers east of Havana the small fishing port of Cojímar – situated at the mouth of the river that gives it its name – specializes in shark-fishing, swordfish, marlin and dolphin by "trolling", was not directly accessible from La Habana Vieja until the tunnel under the bay was built in 1957. So Hemingway often moored the *Pilar* in the basins of Casablanca, La Regla, Arsenal or San Francisco. To get to Cojímar from La Habana Vieja he had to go round the Enseñada de Guanabacoa by the Los Ángeles district, before taking the Carretera at Guanabacoa, which led him to the town of the same name and allowed him to reach the Carretera at Cojímar. Setting out from San Francisco de Paula, he followed the Carretera to Güines, went by Lucero then Jacomino and had the choice of two routes: he could go directly to Guanabacoa by the Carretera or pass by San Miguel del Padron. Today, the tunnel puts Cojímar only about ten kilometers away from Havana.

The little village hardly seems to have changed: a few low houses, a few barks, a frail pontoon facing the Torréon, a small colonial fortress going out into the sea, built in the seventeenth century by the Spanish at the same time as **Castillo de la Chorrera** at the mouth of the Almendares, the catholic church with its yellow and white facade. Here and there, old villas with columns and pilasters surrounded by abandoned parks.

When not in his modest dwelling – Calle Pesuela, no. 209, between Buena Vista and Carmen – Gregorio Fuentes never tires of recounting his life with Hemingway at one of the tables of **La Terraza**, the restaurant frequented by Santiago in *The Old Man and the Sea* and by Thomas Hudson in *Islands in the Stream* Aged a little over a hundred, the old sailor from the *Pilar* is one of the last living witnesses to the Hemingway saga.

How moving it is to hear him recounting in great detail how he met Hemingway in 1928 at Dry Tortugas when a strong north-east wind forced them into port and how, from 1938 onward he, the Canary islander who had been a sailor from the age of four, was employed on board the *Pilar!* "Hemingway liked his boat to be well varnished, well painted, nice and clean", he recounts, adding that the great man said *la mar*, in Spanish, in the same way as those who really love it.

Seated at the foot of the belvedere, with its bust of Hemingway dedicated by his fishermen friends who melted down everything bronze or metallic they possessed in order to erect this moving memorial, we find ourselves imagining what life must have been like at Cojímar with Anselmo Hernández, El Sordo, Cachimba, Cheo Lopez and a few others, "men who never went to church and who never consciously dressed as fishermen", inexhaustible sources of inspiration for Hemingway. We think of the Gómez, the *Pilar's* support boat, coasting in front of the fortress, of Spencer Tracy coming to do locations for *The Old Man and the Sea,* of the famous photo where we can see Gregorio Fuentes and Hemingway posing beside a swordfish suspended by the tail, of the cat Boise (the capital of Idaho) found at La Terraza, of "freshly cooked shrimp garnished with lemon and left on the counter", eaten by Thomas Hudson one sunny Christmas morning… We also think of the *balseros* who used Cojímar as their point of departure for Miami.

• **La Terraza.** Calle Real y Candelaria.
Seafood specialties. Here we can meet Gregorio
Fuentes at noon and at dinner time.

Hemingway, on his return from an African safari (1953-1954), poses alongside the white marlin caught by Gregorio Fuentes.

LA HABANA VIEJA

Itinerary 1
Plaza de la Catedral (near la Bodeguita del medio)

Calle Empedrado, originally called "Del" or "El Empedrado" i.e. paved or stoned, takes its name from the *chinas pelonas* (small smooth stones) it was covered with in 1641 to prevent the rain water that trickled down to the port from rendering it impracticable. Famous in the seventeenth century because of the butcher's shop for the soldiers stationed there at the time, then in the nineteenth for Madame Pebaite's Hotel with its baths and dining room, as well as many other "luxurious appointments", today it is largely neglected, like many other streets in La *Habana Vieja*.

To the left of the **Bodeguita del medio**, la **Casa del Conde de la Réunion** – now restored, it houses the **Centro de Promoción Cultural y Museo Carpentier** – is a fine example of eighteenth century Spanish colonial architecture, with its finely worked monumental indoor stairs, patio surrounded by balconies and baroque arcades, as are the **Casa del Marqués de Aguas Claras** (now the **Restaurante El Patio**), **el Palacio de los Marqueses de Arcos** (**Taller Experimental de Grafica de La Habana**), and **el Palacio del Conde Lombillo** (the present **Museo de la Educacion**), built between 1730 and 1746. **El Palacio de los Condes de Casa Bayona**, built in 1720 by the governor of Cuba, which has in turn been the head office of a daily newspaper during the early years of the Republic, then a rum factory, and is now **el Museo de Arte Colonial**. As for the **Antigua Casa de Baños**, built in the nineteenth century on the site of old reservoirs containing drinking water for the ships in the nearby port,

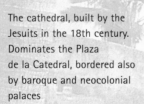

The cathedral, built by the Jesuits in the 18th century. Dominates the Plaza de la Catedral, bordered also by baroque and neocolonial palaces

with its neo-baroque facade built in 1931, it is separated by the callejon de Chorro from the **Casa de San Ignacio**.

Renamed when the cathedral was built, the **Plaza de la Catedral** overlooks the most important monument in the area, the Cathedral. Built by the Jesuits in the eighteenth century and added to several times between 1802 and 1832, its sober "Tuscan" facade conceals a central nave with three adjacent naves and eight side-chapels. The ashes of Christopher Columbus rested there until 1898.

Itinerary 2
Plaza de Armas (around the hotel Ambos Mundos)

Was Hemingway an adept at the art of walking? Without being either Robert Walser or Paul Auster, for whom walking is essentially a matter of metaphysics, we may suppose that he was. Certain pages and testimonies suggest it. The tangled web of streets in La *Habana Vieja*, narrow to prevent the Caribbean sun from penetrating too far, invites us to walk and stroll – or certainly did so in those days. We mustn't forget: Hemingway discovered Havana in the thirties…

From the **Plaza de la Catedral** to the **Plaza de Armas** is only a few steps as they say. From his fifth floor room in the Ambos Mundos hotel Hemingway could see Havana Bay and the port on one side and, on the other, la Plaza de Armas. He cannot fail to have wandered along these libertine, noisy streets thriving with trade.

Between the **Catedral** and the **Casa de Lombrillo**, let's take Calle Empedrado, then the first right, Calle Mercaderes. We come across Calle O'Reilly then Obispo, two mythical and voracious streets that José Cemi, the hero of Paradiso, paces after his siesta in search of a bookshop: "These two streets, in reality they are only one street in two parts: one for going to the bay and the other for going back to town. From one of these streets we seem to follow the light all the way to the sea, then, coming back, in a sort of prolongation of the light, to go from the brightness of the bay to the pith of the elder." At the corner of Mercaderes and Obispo, the **Ambos Mundos** hotel that Hemingway only left to go and live with Martha at the *Finca*.

Let's go down *Calle Obispo*. To the right, several renovated buildings: *Casa de Obispo*, no. 119 (*Oficina del Historiador*), *Museo de Plata*, *Casa de Obispo*, no. 113 (*Dulcena Doña Teresa, Barbería*) and, to finish, at the crossroads with Oficios, **la Casa de Obispo y Oficios (Restaurante La Mina, Casa del Agua la Tinaja,**

The Palacio de los Capitanes Generales, as seen from room 525 at the hotel Ambos Mundos.

Hotel Ambos Mundos, At the corner of Calle Obispo and Mercaderes. The corner room on the top storey is the one occupied by Hemingway.

Palacio de los Capitanes Generales. Occupies the west side of the Plaza de Armas. The colored *mediapuntos* filter the light.

the end of the nineteenth century. Lastly, we mustn't forget the **Castillo de la Real Fuerza**, Calle O'Reilly, with its tower, added in 1632, surmounted with the Giraldilla, a bronze figure representing the wife of Hernando de Soto, symbol of the city. Finally, at no. 7 Calle Obispo stands an imposing building, formerly the United States Embassy, its location no longer figures on any map of La Habana Vieja. Now it is destined to become the future **Biblioteca provincial de Educación Rubén Martínez Villena**. "Inside", writes Hemingway "you were supposed to fill out your name and address and the object of your visit at a table where a sad clerk with plucked eyebrows and a moustache across the extreme lower part of his upper lip looked up and pushed the paper towards him."...

Itinerary 3
Parque Central (around the Floridita)

Let's take Calle Obispo yet again, now gutted, formerly luxurious. In *Islands in the Stream,* Thomas Hudson-Hemingway goes down it "a thousand times in the daytime and in the night." He did not like to ride down it for it was over too quickly.

At the end of Calle Obispo, which means "Bishop" street, **El Floridita**, in what we might call the area of the **Parque Central**, going from the **Capitolio Nacional** (today's **Museo de Ciencias Naturales**), a copy of the Washington Capitol inaugurated in 1929, and ending at the foot of the **Castillo de San Salvador de la Punta**, twin brother of the **Castillo de los Tres Reyes del Morro**, constructed on the other side of the channel for the purpose of defending The Bay of Havana.

Heladería El Anón, Café Habanero). Facing the Plaza de Armas, the oldest, still paved with wood on the west side, the **Palacio de los Capitanes Generales**, in late Baroque style. It was the presidential palace from 1902 to 1920. Today it houses the **Museo de la Ciudad.** To the left, the **Palacio del Segundo Cabo**, with a superb inner patio, formerly the palace of the Poste and built in 1770. Opposite, behind the statue of Manuel de Cespedes, the "father of the country", erected in 1954 by Batista to replace the statue of King Ferdinand VII, the **Templete**, the first neoclassical edifice (1828) in Havana, based on a Greco-Doric model and decorated inside with paintings by the French painter David Vermay, founder of the Academia de Pintura y Dibujo de San Alejandro. To the south west of the square, the Palacio de **Los Condes de Santovenía**, built at the end of the eighteenth century by the brothers Francisco and Nicolás Martínez de Campo, has been the **hotel Santa Isabel** since

The way down to the sea, the departure point of the **Malecón**, is by the **Prado** – renamed paseo de Martí. Designed by the marquis de la Torre in 1772, it was the aristocratic avenue until the twenties. The way back up to the Floridita will take us along the Avenida Bélgica (Montserrate).

Neglecting the faded charms of the old paseo with its shaded stone benches and art deco street lamps reflecting the shadow of the barouche transporting Cecilia Valdés, the sensual mulatto girl in "The Hill of the Angel", Cirilo Villaverde's novel, we pass in front of the **Monumento a los Estudiantes de Medicina** followed by the **Monumento al General Máximo Gómez** before coming to this avenue where we can see the **"Gramma" Memorial** containing the yacht on which Fidel Castro arrived in December 1956 at Playa las Coloradas. The **Museo de la Revolución** now occupies a neoclassical palace that was the official residence of the presidents of the Cuban Republic until 1960. And lastly, the **Museo Nacional de Bellas Artes**, where we can admire the masterpieces of Cuban painting and particularly certain works by Antonio Gattorno, defended by Hemingway in Esquire: "Spain is an open wound on the right arm that is not healing; Cuba is another; a nice ulcer on the left arm."

Sloppy Joe's (252, Agramonte/Zulueta) has now disappeared. Nothing remains but the facade, but other Hemingway haunts have lived on: the **Plaza hotel**, the **Sevilla hotel** and the **Inglaterra hotel**, neighbor to the **Gran Teatro de La Habana**, the famous building in Spanish neo-gothic style, built in 1915, which welcomed Sarah Bernhardt, Enrico Caruso, Claudia Muzzio, Erich Kleiber and many others. Today it is home to the **Ballet Nacional de Cuba**. Lastly, worth noting, still on Bélgica (Montserrate), between Empedrado and Progreso, **Emilio Baccardi's tropical art deco building** with its central tower surmounted by a black bat said to have inspired Bob Kane, comic strip author and rum lover.

• **Bibliography**: *Guia de la Ciudad Habana*. Ediciónes Gianni Costantino, 1994.

The Edificio Baccardi. Avenida de Bélgica, between San Juan de Dios and Empedrado. An art deco building built in the 1930's.

HOTELS

The most chic hotel in Havana is still the **Nacional**, this old neo-colonial-style palace built in the Vedado district by the Mafia. With its central aisle framed by palm trees, its two clock towers, two swimming pools and bar overlooking the bay and the Malecón, it charmed Errol Flynn and Ava Gardner, Marlon Brando, Winston Churchill, Frank Sinatra, and, more recently, Régine Deforges... But Ernest M. Hemingway never went there.

Hemingway frequented five hotels. The **Hostal Valencia**, in *La Habana Vieja*. This old eighteenth century palace has a pretty Andalusian-style patio, gallery corridors and twelve spacious high-ceilinged bedrooms. Hemingway is said to have occupied (the experts differ, some even saying he never set foot there...) room 21. Founded in 1875, the **hotel Inglaterra** is a neoclassical palace in the Arabo-Andalusian style. Considered to be the oldest hotel in Havana, it has old-world charm, but also 84 air-conditioned rooms and a magnificent terrace from which to discover the Capitol district. Situated on the Prado, a few steps from the museum home of Lezama Lima, but also from the Floridita, from *La Habana Vieja* and Calle Obispo, the **hotel Sevilla** was praised by Paul Morand in Hiver Caraïbe and Graham Greene who, in *Our Man in Havana*, had room 510 occupied by a certain Wormold. The **Plaza hotel** is also situated a few yards from the location of the old walls of Habana Vieja. It is well worth a visit, with its marble fountain, terrace, Belle époque hall and 1900 frills. Juan, the chauffeur, went there to get the papers that Hemingway read every day in the Floridita bar. The last hotel is the **Ambos Mundos**. Hemingway stayed there whenever he visited Havana, from 1932 to 1939, in the famous room 525 on the fifth floor, "this marvelous place to work without a telephone", which has now been turned into a museum.

- **Hotel Nacional**. Corner Calle 0 and 21.
- **Hostal Valencia**. Corner Calle Oficios and Obrapìa.
- **Hotel Inglaterra**. Prado no. 416, corner with San Rafael.
- **Hotel Sevilla**. Calle Trocadero, no. 55, corner with Prado.
- **Hotel Plaza**. Calle Ignacio Agramonte, n°. 267.
- **Hotel Ambos Mundos**. Corner Calle Obispo and Mercaderes.

BOOKSHOPS

"Cemí woke up from his siesta wanting to go out to Obispo and O'Reilly to visit the bookshops..." Just like the emblematic character of *Paradiso*, Hemingway liked to stroll through the bookshops in *La Habana Vieja* which, at the time, were flourishing. We only have to stroll through these streets to find the traces, essentially signs and worn old facades, of this bookish past.

At the corner of Obispo and Bernaza stands a shuttered buil-

ding that once housed the biggest bookshop in Havana, La **Moderna Poesía**, founded in 1898 and still booming when Hemingway took this section of Calle Obispo to walk to the Floridita. The group Cultural S. A., "Empresa librera y editora", founded in 1926, of which La Moderna Poesía was part, also included La **Librería Cervantes**, as well as departments for gifts, perfumes, hardware, paper, sports articles, office equipment and maintenance equipment for typewriters of the Remington Rand group. In 1944 José López Serrano and Ricardo Veloso Guerra employed 536 people!

There are no longer any large bookshops in Havana but a string of **secondhand bookshops**. We find many along Obispo but also fixed stalls on the Plaza de Armas and at the Feria fair that is held at the far end of the Vedado, between Malecón and the Avenida de los Presidentes, a fine gathering of knowledgeable – secondhand book dealers selling their own collections or those of others… Lovers of old books will think themselves in paradise. Next to beautifully bound books by nineteenth century French authors (any self-respecting Latin American intellectual had some on his bookshelves) and first edition texts by García Lorca, Miguel Hernández, Manuel Altolaguirre or copies of the review Origenes, you can find, a hotchpotch on the subject that interests us, fascinating Guías Sociales de La Habana dating from before 1959, a Habana Antigua with maps and sketches published in 1875, a copy of the very rare and now

Hall of the Hotel Ambos Mundos. Before it was renovated in 1997, the ground floor had been converted to a garage.

Façade of the Hotel Sevilla. Frequented by Paul Morand and Graham Greene.

Dining room of the Hotel Sevilla. Situated on the top floor, it dominates the whole town.

There are countless Cuban editions of Hemingway's books. This is the cover of an edition of Fiesta published in 1971.

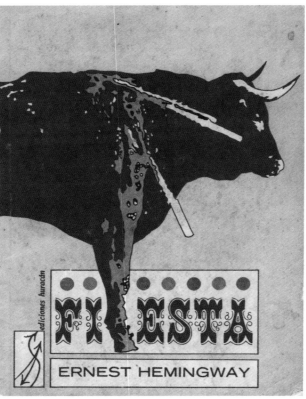

Miramar Beach in the 1950's. Avenida 5, named after the famous avenue in New York, runs through the Miramar quarter, which is today still the chic area in Havana. It starts at Malecón and finishes at Hemingway Marina.

out of print *Fishes of Cuba and the Atlantic Coasts of Tropical America*, by the eminent Carlos de la Torre y Huerta, old tourist guidebooks published between the twenties and fifties and aimed at Americans who wanted to find out about Cuba, and lastly, of course, a vast collection of literature devoted to Ernest Hemingway. The classics (*Hemingway in Cuba*, by Norberto Fuentes; *Cuba y Hemingway en el Gran Rio Azul*, by Mary Cruz) and more recent works like *Un personaje llamado Hemingway*, by Claudio Izquierdo Funcia. Or, if we really search, old reviews containing articles devoted to Hemingway: El Mundo, Alerta, Prensa Libre, Gente, Carteles, Union... And, of course, old editions of Hemingway texts translated into Spanish and published by Ediciones Huracán or by the Editora del Consejo nacional de Cultura, including the famous *El Viejo y el mar: "Era un viejo que pescaba solo en un bote en el Gulf Stream et hacía ochenta y cuatro días que no cogí un pez..."*

MIRAMAR

To the west of the cemetery of Colón, the Vedado ends at the river Almendares. On the other side is Miramar, for a long time, until the tunnel was built, accessible by means of a bridge starting from Calle 7 and continuing into Avenida 5, a name chosen by millionaire Americans who moved here in the twenties as a reference to New York's famous Fifth Avenue. A guidebook from the thirties describes this district as being in all ways comparable to the "famous bois de Boulogne", that the proximity of the sea, trees laden with tropical fruit, dance halls and large avenues make it a sort of Cuban Champs-élysées.

For a very long time Miramar was and, in certain respects, still is the chic district of Havana. Here and there splendid colonial-style villas dating from the thirties or fifties, surrounded by carefully tended gardens, house celebrities of the régime, diplomats and are the seat of many embassies. The Country Club, Oriental Park, Nacional Casino and Marianao Beach, the playground of the American underground and rich Cubans, have now disappeared. What remains is a strangely lunar district that awaits some indefinite future, like the turtles of the **Aquarium Nacional** (corner 60th and First Avenue) among the cascading tropical plants, bougainvillea, hibiscus and palm trees with smooth trunks, while the sea, still very close, offers up its cargo of salt and wind.

MUSIC

As we saw in the section devoted to the *Finca Vigía,* Ernest Hemingway's tastes in this domain were highly eclectic. His record collection does not have one single record of Cuban

music, which is something of an exploit since music is absolutely everywhere. Alejo Carpentier rightly states that Cuban music is "the essence of rhythm, sun and life" (Chronicles). But he is not the only one to consider music as one of the main identifying features of Cuban-ness. Nicolás Guillén makes many references to it in his *Paginas vueltas*. And Federico García Lorca, when asked by a journalist what impressed him most about Cuba, did not hesitate to reply "Its music. When I finished my conferences I stayed on to study the music." (*Complete Works*, vol. II.)

Habanera, guarija, bolero, danzón, guaracha, son, pregon, punto, conga, mambo, cha-cha-cha, charanga, boolagoo, mozambique, cucaracha, salsa – just a small example of the Cuban sounds that haunt the streets, hotel corridors, restaurants, patios, cafés and houses. Cuba is one of the rare Latin American countries to possess a lively tradition of academic music and an inventive and energetic corps de ballet. And we mustn't forget the very strong influence of Cuban sounds on jazz music. As early as the forties, Arsenio Rodríguez (inventor of the *montuno* sound), the group Sonora Matancera in the fifties, not to mention Beny Moré and bass player Israel López established the reputation of Cuban jazz. Today's music: Company Segundo and Rubén González.

- **Palacio de Artesanía** (Tienda Chaplin).
Calle 23, between 10 and 12, Vedado.
- **Egrem.**
Calle Campanario, between Neptuno and San Miguel, Centro.
- **Casa de la Música.**
20 and 35, Miramar.
- **Museo Nacional de la Música.**
Calle Capdevilla, n°.1, between Habana and Aguiar,
La Habana Vieja.

PALM TREES

The palm tree is the king of the eight thousand vegetal species listed in Cuba. The island is said to have as many as 70 million palm trees… We find them absolutely everywhere. In the savanna, the cane sugar fields, on the flanks of the hills and along the banks of the rivers, serving as perches for the tiny hummingbirds of the Sierra del Rosario and as a provisional hiding place for the deer of Pinar del Rio. But we also find them in the center of patios in La Habana Vieja, at the foot of fortresses, framing certain ostentatious mauso-

leums of the Colón cemetery, highlighting the profile of a baroque church and obviously in profusion at the '*Finca Vigía.*' The fourteen acres of grounds contain many different species, with the exception of the very rare Hyerocyas calocoma, which dates from prehistory and can still be found in the province of Pinar del Rio. Hemingway and Mary Welsh, who paid very special attention to the flora of the property, lived amidst an explosion of flowers, tropical plants and royal palm trees with whitish gray trunks and bright green branches shaken by the wind. (*Islands in the Stream*).

Jardin botánico.
Carretera Rocio (20 kilometers south west of Havana).

There are over 70 million palm trees in Cuba. The most famous are the Royal palms.

FISHING

There are three types of fishing in Cuba: fresh water fishing (for trout and perch), skin diving (at Île de la Jeunesse and Cayo del Sur) and deep-sea fishing with heavy and sophisticated equipment. It was the third kind that attracted Hemingway to the Florida strait in 1928. The presence of the warm current of the Gulf Stream attracts many fish that use it as a crossing point, a spawning and reproduction ground: tarpon, marlin, shark, grenadier, manta, mackerel, barracuda, bonefish – all abound in its waters.

Catching big fish is a demanding and difficult sport that requires tenacity and intelligence. It is not unusual to have to fight for more than an hour with fish that, like marlin or swordfish, can weigh over four hundred pounds, They are governed, according to some, by the full moon and execute very curious dances: "These fish eat more at the full moon. Also, where the current is strong is where the fish bite most. Marlin and swordfish swim on their sides in a zigzag. Every two or three hundred yards they turn and go against the current to prevent the water from entering their gills." (Carlos Soldevilla, *Cuba*) This combat with the fish is part of the fishing tradition in Cuba. Hemingway was not inspired to write *The Old Man and the Sea* by any one particular man but, as Mary Cruz (*Cuba y Hemingway en el Gran Río Azul*) points out, comes directly from a tradition of daily struggle: the struggle of the poor fishermen on the north coast of Cuba. It is nothing new. In an article published in June 1891 in La Habana Elegante, Ramón Meza was already exalting the virile qualities of the fisherman, "this hero who each day conducts an obscure and resigned struggle to survive".

Hemingway was a true professional fisherman. The fishermen made him one of their own by creating a competition that is named after him. He devised part of the rules. The first competition was held at Cojímar in 1950. The Miramar Yacht Club won it the first year and the Habana Biltmore the second… It still exists and takes place the second fortnight of May because the best season for deep-sea fishing is, approximately, May to June.

The **Hemingway Marina**, a vast tourist zone that receives hundreds of yachts along its three miles of canals, now organizes many tournaments: **the Sailing and Curricán tournaments** (second fortnight in April), **the Ernest Hemingway tournament**, the **Spring tournament**, **the Blue Marlin tournament and the Castero tournament** (second fortnight in August). It goes without saying that Hemingway never set foot in any of these places except the entrance to the Marina where we have the small fishing village of Jaimanitas… There are other tournaments, but from November to April, at Playas del Este, Cayo Largo and on the cayos in the province of Ciego de Avila. The **Marina Tarará**, near Cojimar, enjoys the distinction of having been visited by Hemingway and his '*Pilar.*' It also organizes fishing tournaments: the **torneo de la Hispanidad**, from October 10 to 14, the torneo Cuba-Canaria, in mid February, and the **torneo El Viejo y el Mar**, in July. To get a better understanding of Hemingway's passion for fishing, it is imperative to visit the **Museo de Ciencias Felipe-Poey** (**Academia de Ciencias de Cuba**). Alongside collections of birds, mammals and insects, etc., the "greatest Cuban naturalist", Don Felipe Poey y Aloy, has assembled an impressive collection of marine species.

RESTAURANTS

Hemingway makes many culinary references throughout his work. He enjoys eating and he says so. In *Across the River and Into the Trees* the colonel declares his love to the young woman over a locally made crab enchillada while advising her to drink a good white wine with her mixed grill. We remember the plate "of little pieces of pork, fried and crunchy" and the plate of "red perch fried in batter so that the reddish-pink skin was enrobed in a yellow crust inside", served to Thomas Hudson at the Floridita, and the dish of avocados with vinaigrette sauce and banded rudderfish savored by the crew of the *Pilar* on another trip.

Hemingway on board the '*Pilar*'. A swordfish can weigh several hundred pounds and requires a struggle of perhaps half a day before being finally landed.

The home pont of the *Pilar* was Cojimar, but the boat also mooned at Tarará, Jaimanitas, Baracoa, Mariel, Puerto Escondido, etc.

Kenneth Tynan, a guest at the *Finca,* describes a meal: "the starter, a large salad bowl of icebiche, shellfish seasoned with a vinaigrette, followed by grilled bass with fennel. Then came the fruit, then a black coffee. Between two mouthfuls Hemingway held forth in masterly fashion." (Holiday, February 1960).

Cuban culinary art is a combination of Spanish and African dishes that, in the nineteenth century, gave birth to Creole cooking. Slightly spiced, and overall quite simple, Cuban cuisine has its classics: *moros y cristianos* (rice accompanied by black beans, onions and lardons), *congrí* (rice and beans), *ajiaco* (dried meat and roots). Chicken is used in different dishes, such as *arroz con pollo, pollo con salsa criolla* and *pollo barbacoa*. The plantain banana, el *plátano*, can be prepared in a thousand different ways. We find it in the *picadillo, testones* and *the fufú*... Fish is not part of traditional Cuban cooking, except for *sopa de camarones* (shrimp soup)

and *langosta enchilada* (grilled lobster prepared with chillies and tomatoes). There are many desserts: *boniatillo* (cinnamon flan), *conquimol* (coconut flan), ice cream, *plátano en tentación* (fried banana with sugar and cinnamon).

Although nourishing and stimulating, Cuban cuisine is nevertheless not very varied. But it exudes a certain magic, due perhaps to the consummate cooking skills that always accompany a very judicious use of the ingredients.

Curiously, the guidebooks from the period between the thirties and the fifties very rarely include a chapter entitled "food preparation and presentation"... Sometimes Hemingway ate at **the Shangai**, which was also an opium den and a bordello and which has of course disappeared today. As well as at **La Bodeguita del medio** and **the Floridita**. The former remains, whatever else one might say about it, a good restaurant offering excellent Creole cooking. As for the latter, the fish and seafood are less well-known than the cocktails served at the bar... The majority of the large hotels offer an insipid international cuisine to the sound of howling bands. The **Roof Garden of the Sevilla Hotel** offers nothing more than a beautiful view of Havana. The roof garden of the **Inglaterra Hotel** adds the most edible of fish. To encounter Cuban warmth, friendliness and good, authentic cooking we must go to *paladares*, tiny and charming privately owned restaurants. Yam purée at the **Paladar Estrela**, Creole cuisine at the **Trinidad Colonial**, magic fish at the **Bistrot** (on the Malecón), and most of all, **La Guarida**, the last "tematico" restaurant still fashionable, situated in the apartment where the famous *Fresa y Chocolate* was shot, a film we can rent on the spot (Calle Concordia, no. 418. corner Gervasio and Escobar)... Lastly, we mustn't forget Cuban sandwiches: *pierna, pollo* and *queso*, served on triangular slices of warm bread. The best are those of the **Nacional Hotel**, served under the palm trees facing the sea.

RUM

Rón is the Cuban national drink. More perfumed and less powerful than Antilles rum, Cuban rum is divided into three main types depending on its age: *carta blanca* (clear, light and dry, often used in cocktails, three years old), *carto oro* (amber-colored, with golden tones, five years old), *anejo* (dark amber in color, it is aged in wood and drunk with ice and sparkling water or *la roca*, seven years old). We can also find white rum (caña) and *extra-seco* (a slightly golden rum

A house on the road leading to San Fransisco de Paula, a village situated ten miles south west of Havana, where Hemingway lived from 1939 till he left Cuba in July 1960.

The *Pilar*. On Hemingwayís death, Mary Welsh asked Gregorio Fuentes to scuttle her in the open sea off Havana. Abandoned at the far end of the port she was finally towed ashore and left on dry land under the palm trees at the *Finca Vigía*.

that is produced in limited quantities).

There are many brands (about 80!): Bucanero, Caribbean Club, Rón Varadero, Las Palmas... But the best known are Havana Club (recognizable because of the *giraldilla*, the symbol of Havana, on its label) and Baccardi. Produced outside Cuba since the Revolution, it is much appreciated by Cubans in Miami.

It would be something of an understatement to say that Hemingway drank a lot. His appetite for liquor was legendary. Milt Machlin, a guest at the *Finca* in July 1958, recounts that while in the Floridita he put his capacity to absorb alcohol to the test by "tasting" several Papa's specials. "Did you reach my record" replied Hemingway. How many? answered the journalist. – Fifteen specials!"

Any self-respecting Cuban barman knows at least a hundred cocktails and the hotel school, created in 1960, includes a course entitled "the art of the barman". There are any number of rum cocktails: baracao especial, Cuba libre, daiquiri, Henry Morgan, mulata, piña colada, presidente, ron Collins, saoco...There are two which have direct links with Hemingway: the Hemingway special and the *mojito*. The recipe for the first: 4 ounces of Havana Club Light Dry, 2 spoons of *toronja* (citron) juice, 1 spoon of maraschino, 1 lime, crushed ice, "batase and sirvase frapé..." The recipe for the second: place two ice cubes in a conical glass, add the juice of one lemon, 1/2 spoon of sugar, 2 drops Angostura bitters, 2 ounces of Havana Club Light Dry, sparkling water and a sprig of *yerbabuena* (a sort of mint).

But Cubans don't drink only rum. Their pale ale is very much appreciated (Cristal and Hatuey – the latter figured prominently in the iceboxes of the *Pilar*), as are the fruit-based *batidos* (non alcoholic), small cups of strong and very black coffee, and the *guarapo*, a clear juice extracted from cane sugar and served with or without rum.

- **Casa del Rón**. Calle Baratillo, n°.53, between Obispo and Montserrate, Habana Vieja.
- **Floridita.** The temple of the Hemingway special. But also to buy or drink the Solera Centenario (rum that has been aged for more than sixty years).
- **Bodeguita del medio**. The mojito is quite disappointing.
- **INTUR boutiques of the Habana Libre hotels, Riviera, Sevilla**.
- **The bar of the Nacional** Hotel. For its excellent mojito.

SAN FRANCISCO DE PAULA

Situated about nine miles south east of Havana, the little locality of San Francisco de Paula derives its name from the Canary islander Agustín Francisco de Arocha who in 1774 favored the construction of the San Francisco de Paula hermitage, around which a village quickly developed. In the Diccionario geográfico, estadístico, histórico de la Isla de Cuba we read: "San Francisco de Paula (village). Situated about four leagues to the west of Santa María del Rosario on high uneven ground on the northern flank of the Baccalao hill and extending to the banks of the río Luyanó. Of a pleasing appearance it consists of 26 houses and 141 inhabitants of all ages, sexes and colors. It has a stone hermitage built in 1795 by Don Francisco Arocha." When Hemingway moved there it had hardly changed. There is a village festival on the 2nd of April each year, the hypothetical date of its foundation. Boundary conflicts were commonplace.

Although it is thought that the *Finca Vigía* takes its name from a tower formerly erected by the Spanish, we do not know the exact date of its construction. The famous ceiba to the right of the main entrance must have been between 150 and 200 years old when Hemingway rented the property (prior to buying it) from Joseph D'Orn Duchamp, a French property owner. The ad that appeared in the Havanese Social review said: "Villa to rent from May to October, la *Finca Vigía,* at San Francisco de Paula. Light, telephone, water, etc. Train every hour. Paved road to entrance to house. One of the most pleasant residences in Havana. To visit, please telephone." The rest is history. *La Finca Vigía,* is an identical replica of the house at 907 Whitehead Street in Key West, which Hemingway left one December day in 1939 at

the wheel of his new Buick… He moved in there with Martha and later lived there with Mary.

- **Museo Ernest-Hemingway.** San Francisco de Paula. Open every day from 9:00 a.m. to 4:00 p.m. and Sundays from 9:00 a.m. to 1:00 p.m. Closed on Tuesdays and rainy days.

SANTERÍA

Santería is the Cuban equivalent of voodoo in Haiti or macumba in Brazil. An astonishing blend of Catholicism and African religions, it was introduced by the slaves who, faced with the ban on practicing their own religions, chose to hide their gods behind the saints of Christian mythology. Saint Barbe was thus associated with Chango, Saint Francis of Assisi with Orula. Ogun is Saint Peter and Oddua is Jesus, etc. Hemingway could not have been indifferent to this animistic tradition with its divinities, called *orishas*, deriving their existence from nature: rivers, storms, the sea, lightning, wind, etc. Here and there, scattered throughout his life and work, signs appear, a few references. In *No One Ever Dies* the black man with the straw hat is afraid at the end of the story and wraps his fingers around the blue seeds of the voodoo beads that he holds tightly. But this was not enough to calm his fear, Hemingway adds, because this time he was up against a much older magic. There are other clues… The Nobel Prize medal that he placed in 1954 at the feet of the Virgin de la Caridad del Cobre, patron saint of Cuba, who is none other than Ochún, goddess of fresh water, symbol of sensuality and love. Or his frequent journeys to the Regla district, on the other side of Havana Bay, to join the *Pilar*, docked in the shade of the church of the Santísima Virgen de Regla, patron saint of Havana fishermen, a black Virgin holding a white infant Jesus, she is assimilated with Yemay·, the black goddess of the sea, symbol of life.

In *Hemingway Rediscovered*, Norberto Fuentes recounts that Lucia Castillo Cabrera, the wife of Juan Pastor, the chauffeur, told him that in her opinion "the American believed", which in the Cuban vernacular meant that he was a *santería* adept. She remembered a day when Hemingway, knowing she was ill, advised Juan to take her to see "a person", a *santero* in San Francisco de Paula. To be treated she had to dress all in white. Hemingway paid from his own pocket the thousand dollars demanded by the priest-healer. On another occasion, she recalled Hemingway returning

from Africa (1953) and announcing that he had "got married". Worried that a son might be born to him and wanting to respect the rites of the wakamba, he asked his doctor to pierce his earlobes "before the little fellow is born in Africa" in order to be able to wear the ritual rings. But the most disturbing fact of all was his violent reaction when he surprised Mary and the gardener cutting up the roots of the ceiba that was pushing up the paving stones on the patio of the *Finca*. The ceiba is a sacred tree in Santeria and it is forbidden to mutilate it or even cut it down… The root hanging over the door to the guest bedroom was not, as some claim, a ceiba root, but the root of a mangle rojo (red mangrove).

- **Church of the Santísima Virgen de Regla**. Regla. Access by means of a lancha from La Habana Vieja (on Desamprados San Pedro).
- **Guanabacoa Municipal History Museum.** The Mecca of santeria. Guanabacoa. Calle Martí, n°. 108, between Versales and San Antonio.

The church of Santisima Virgen de Regla. La Regla is the centre of Cuban santeria. Patron Saint of Sailors and of Havana, the statue of the Black Madonna of Regla holds a white infant Jesus in her arms. According to Lucia Castillo Cabrera, the wife of Juan Pastor, Hemingway's chauffeur, Ernest was a follower of the santería: "the American believed," he used to say.

The patio of the *Finca Vigía*.

The places Hemingway and his characters frequented in Havana

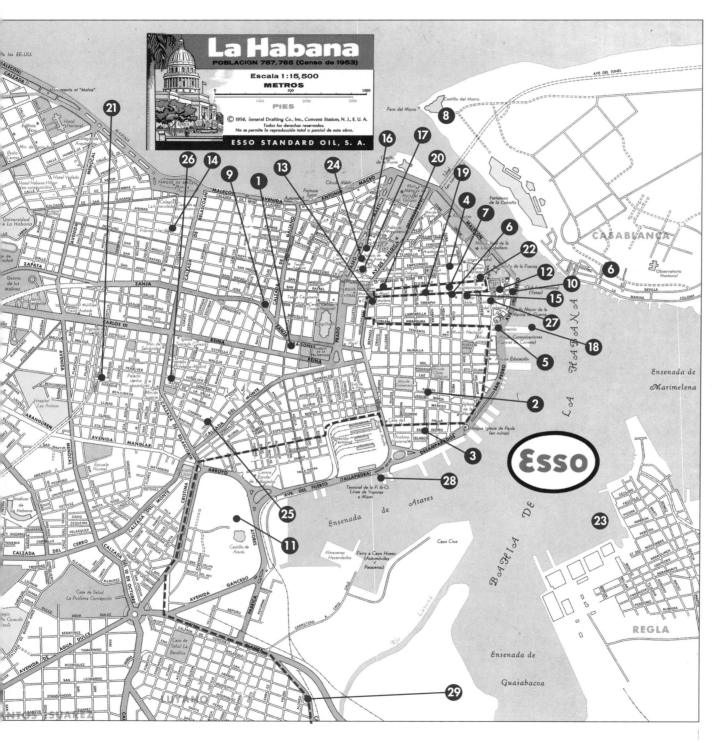

1. Banco Nacional de Cuba (calle Amistad, 420)
2. Barrio de Jesús María
3. Barrio de San Isidro
4. Bodeguita del Medio
5. Café de La Perla (Muelle San Francisco), Bar Cunard (Oficios, 32), Plaza de la Fuente
6. Casablanca
7. Casa Recalt (between Cuba and San Ignacio, on Obispo)
8. Castle Morro
9. Centro Vasco
10. Club Naútico International
11. Cuartel de San Ambrosio
12. Embajada Norteamericana (Obispo, 7)
13. Floridita
14. Fronton Jai-Alai
15. Hôtel Ambos Mundos (Obispo, 153, on the corner with Mercaderes)
16. Hôtel Sevilla (trocadero, 55)
17. Hôtel Plaza (Parque central, corner Neptuno and Zulueta)
18. Muelle de Luz
19. Calle Obispo
20. Et. Lastra (calle O'Reilly, 506)
21. El Pacífico
22. Papelería
23. Regla
24. Sloppy Joe's (Agramonte/Zulueta, 252)
25. Club Cazadores del Cerro
26. Le Shangaï
27. Hostal valencia (oficios, 53, corner with Obrapía)
28. Linea de Vapores de Miami
29. The route Hemingway and Thomas Hudson (*Islands in the Stream*) took San Francisco de Paula to the Floridita in *Habana Vieja*.

Bibliography

Titles printed in bold contain references to Havana, Cuba and fishing in the Gulf Stream

Fifty Grand
Death in the Afternoon
For Whom the Bell Tolls
To Have and Have Not
The Old Man and the Sea
A Moveable Feast
Across the River and into the Trees
Islands in the Stream
The Nick Adams Stories
The Garden of Eden
The Dangerous Summer
88 Poems - contains 'To Crazy Christian'
Byline - selected articles and dispatches of Four Decades, Touchstone
The Torrents of Spring
A Farewell to Arms
The Sun Also Rises
A Moveable Feast
Death in the Afternoon - Spain and bullfighting
The Green Hills of Africa - African safaris, Depression in America, fishing and storms in the Carribean
Across the River and Into the Trees
Nobel prize acceptance speech
Le Bon Petit Lion, Gallimard
Le Taureau fidèle, Gallimard
Défense du titre, Belfond, 1992 – Interviews selected and presented by Matthew J. Bruccoli. Many of these interviews and sketches are about Cuba

Critical studies on Hemingway

Asselineau (Roger), éd. *The Literary Reputation of Hemingway in Europe, Paris and New York*, Lettres Modernes & New York University Press, 1965.
Astre (Gilbert-A), *Hemingway par lui-meme*, Paris, Le Seuil, 1959.
Baez (Luis), 'Hemingway siempre estuvo a favor de la revolucion', interview with Mary Hemingway, **La Habana, Bohemia, September 1977.**
Baker (Sheridan), Ernest Hemingway – *An Introduction and Interpretation*, New York, Winston and Company, 1967.
Beebe (Maurice), (under the direction of), *Configuration critique d'Ernest Hemingway*, Lettres modernes, 1957.
Burgess (Anthony), *Ernest Hemingway and His World*,

New York, Charles Scribner's Sons 1978.
Boudet (Rosa Ileana), *Hemingway: siempre La Habana*, La Habana, Cuba Internacional, December 1969.
Boulay (Daniel), *La Philosophie du divertissement et de la violence chez Hemingway*, Lille, Université de Lille III, 1972.
Cabrera Infante (Guillermo), *El Viejo y la Marca*, La Habana, Ciclon, September 1956.
Campoamor (Fernando G.), *La vida cubanan de Ernest Hemingway*, La Habana, Bohemia, 21st July 1967.*Circuito Hemingway*, La Habana, 1980.
Cirules (Enrique), *Conversacion con el ultimo norteamericano*, La Habana, Instituto Cubano del Libro, 1973.
Cruz (Mary), *Cuba y Hemingway en el Gran Rio Azul*, La Habana Union de Escritores y Artistas de Cuba, 1981.
Desnoes (Edmundo), *La casa de Hemingway*, La Habana Mayito, April 1965.
Escarpit (Robert), *Hemingway*, Paris, La Renaissance du livre, 1964.
Fitzgerald-Hemingway Annual. Started in 1969, Microcard Editions.
Fuentes (Norberto), *Hemingway en Cuba*, La Habana, Editorial Letras Cubanas, 1984.
Fuentes (Norberto), *Ernest Hemingway*, Paris, Gallimard, 1987.
Gonzalez Bermejo (Ernesto), *Los pescadores de Hemingway*, La Habana, Cuba, September 1962.
Greffin (Peter), *Ernest Hemingway*, Paris, Gallimard, 1985. Collection of articles, including ones by John Brown, Michel del Castillo, Michel Mohrt and Jorge Semprun, Paris, Hachette, 1966.
Hemingway (Gregory, H.), *Hemingway: Papa, A Personal Memoir*, Boston Books, 1976.
Hemingway (Mary Walsh), *How It Was*, New York, Knopf, 1976.
Hemingway Notes : a review devoted to Hemingway (Ohio Northern University, 1971-1980), which became, in 1981, *The Hemingway Review* (Ohio Northwestern University).
Hily-Mane (Geneviève), *Le Vieil Homme et la mer* (literary criticism), Paris, Foliothèque Gallimard, 1991.
Hotchner (A.E.), *Papa Hemingway*, Charles Scribner, 1955.
Izquierdo Funcia (Claudio), *Un personaje llamado Hemingway*, La Habana, Ediciones Mec Graphic Ltd, 1955.
Kert (Bernice), *The Hemingway Women*, New York, Norton, 1983.

Lania (Leo), *Hemingway*, Hachette, 1963.
Lunes de Revolucion – Literary supplement to Revolucion, including texts by Edmundo Desnoes, **Guillermo Cabrera Infante, Lolo Soldevilla and others, 14th August, 1961.**
Manning (Robert), *Hemingway in Cuba*, The Atlantic Monthly, August 1965.
McLendon (James), *Papa Hemingway in Key West*, Miami, E.A. Seeman Publishing, 1972.
Otero (Lisandro), *Hemingway*, La Habana, Casa de las Américas, 1963.
Peterson, (Richard, K.), Hemingway, *Direct and Oblique*, La Haye and Paris, Mouton, 1969.
Mellow (James R.), *Hemingway*, Paris, editions du Rocher, 1995.
Meyers (Jeffrey), *Hemingway*, Paris, Belfond, 1987.
Paporov (Youri), *Pilar*, Moscow, Russia, 1975, *Hemingway ne Kybe*, Moscow, Russia, 1979.
Ritzen (Quentin), *Hemingway*, Paris, Editions Universitaires, 1962.
Sanford (Marcelline Hemingway), *At the Hemingway, A Family Portrait*, Boston, Little, Brown and Company, 1962.
Suarez (Silvano), *El esqueleto del leopardo*, La Habana, 1955.
Vasquez-Candela (Euclides), *Hemingway se preocupa por Cuba y por Fidel*, La Habana, La Gaceta de Cuba, February 1963.
Young (Philip), *Ernest Hemingway – A Reconsideration*, University Park and Londres, Pennsylvania State University Press, 1966.

Appendices

A Cat in the Rain 95
A Clean, Well-Lighted Place 122
Across the River and into the Trees 12, 47, 71, 94, 96, 97, 137, 160
Aguilar León, Luis 47
Anderson, Sherwood 65
Anita (boat) 19, 49, 110
Antigua Casa de Baños 153
Antonelli, Juan Batista 106
After the Storm 14
Arenas, Renaldo 38, 40
Argosy 88
Arguelles, Elicio 84
Atlantic Monthly 68, 139, 149
Autrement, "Cuba" 40, 44
Autrement, La Havane "1952-1961" 41
Autrement, La Havane "1952-1964" 47
Avant la nuit 40
Ayón, Félix 148
Baker, Carlos 10
Balzac, Honoré de 65, 120
Bar Basque 43
Bar Cunard 24
Bario Chino 38
Bataille Georges 101
Batista, Fulgencio (Colonel) 34, 35, 38, 46, 47, 48, 49, 52, 114, 132, 147, 155
Beard, Charles A. 65
Bélgica (avenue) 28, 156, 156
Berenson, Bernard 71, 112
Bergman, Ingrid 85, 86, 95
Bishop, John Pale 87
Black Dog 49, 57, 68, 94, 98, 142
Blue Moon 40
Boating Club 14, 24, 143
Bodeguita del medio 40, 41, 48, 148, 149, 153, 161, 162
Borges, Jorge Luis 18
Borgitti, Renata 74
Braden, Spruille 127
Brooks, Alden 65
Brown, George 84
Brown, John 12
Bruce, Otto 62
Buffalo Bill 65
By Line 61, 126, 129, 134
Cabot, John M. 77
Cabrera Infante, Guillermo 28, 38, 40, 43, 46, 48, 150
Café Cantante 150
Café de La Perla 24
Café de Paris 148
Calmer, Ned 86
Canyon Run Boulevard 52
Capitol (quarter) 22, 156
Capitolio Nacional 22
Carnera, Primo 121
Carol, Martine 86
Carpentier, Alejo 34, 61, 124, 148, 150, 151, 159
Carretera Central 58, 59, 60, 148

Carribean Winter 9, 32, 157
Cartagenas de Indias 98
Carteles 150
Casa de la Música 159
Casa de Lombrillo 153
Casa de Obispo 153, 155
Casa de San Ignacio 153
Casa del Conde de Réunion 153
Casa del Habano 152
Casa del Marqués de Aguas Claras 153
Casa del Rón 162
Casa Partagás 152
Casa Recalt 24, 148
Casablanca 9, 13, 19, 22, 31, 153
Castillo Cabrera, Lucia 163, 163
Castillo de Atarés 24
Castillo de Cojímar 102, 106, 123
Castillo de la Chorrera 153
Castillo de la Real Fuerza 155
Castillo de los Tres Reyes del Morro 101, 102
Castillo, Michel del 142
Castro, Fidel 48, 52, 54, 132, 134, 147, 156
Castro, Fransisco 82
Catedral Colomb 31
Cavallero, Carmen 64
Cayo Coco 151
Cayo Guillermo 151
Cayo Hueso 10
Cayo Largo 151
Cayo Paraíso 151
Cazadores del Cerro (club) 113, 132, 133, 135
Centro de promoción Cultural 153
Centro Gallego Club 150
Centro Vasco 24
Cerro (quarter) 113, 132
Chambers, Canby and Esther 12
Chroniques 61, 151, 151, 159
Ciro's 24
Clerk Club 150
Clittenden (Colonel) 24
Cojímar 19, 35, 74, 91, 107, 110, 117, 122, 124, 126, 128, 142, 153, 153, 160, 160
Colombus, Christopher 18, 28, 151, 154
Complete Works 77, 159
Conrad, Joseph 126
Cooper, Gary 28, 30, 85, 86, 95
Corona 152
Costello, Franck 35
Crane, Hart 151
Cruz, Mary 158, 160
Cuartel de San Ambrosio 24
Cuba 160
Cuba, Carrefour des Caraïbes 150, 152
Cuba, Socialisme et développement 151
D'Orn, Roger 58
Daily Princetonian 88
Daimier, Paul 70

De Arocha, Agustín Fransisco 58, 162
De Beauvoir, Simone 52
De Falla, Manuel 64
Death in the Afternoon 31, 70, 71, 123, 134, 137
Defense of the Realm 30, 58, 98, 133
Diego, Eliseo 44
Dietrich, Marlene 85, 94, 137
Domingo, Roberto 70
Domínguín, Luis Miguel 95
Don Andrés (aka Black Priest) 84, 116
Don Manuel Osorio Manrique de Zuñiga 70
Donne, John 132
Dos Passos, John 10, 11, 19, 31, 65, 124, 133
Dry Tortugas 153
Duke and Duchess of Windsor 86
Duke, Neville 65
Dumont, René 34, 151
Dunabeita, Juan 129
Dunabeita, Sinsky 84, 116
Dupont de Nemours, Irénée 35
Durant, Jimmy 116
Egrem 159
88 poems 72, 120, 133
El Floridita 149
El Sábado de la Rumba 150
Eliot, T. S. 65
Empredrado (street) 153
Enseñada de Atarés 22, 55
Enseñada de Guanabacoa 153
Epoca 97
Escarpit, Robert 43, 114, 122, 136
Esquire 19, 22, 31, 32, 71, 86, 106, 113, 118, 120, 126, 144, 156
Fangio, Juan Manuel 48, 49
Farewell to Arms 31, 76
Father and Boy 43
Faulkner, William 11, 12, 134
Felipe-Poey Natural Science Museum 22
Fenton, Charles 88
Fifty Grand 35
Finca Vigía 24, 43, 47, 52, 54, 57 à 100, 148-150, 153, 158, 159, 161, 162, 163
Fishes of Cuba and the Atlantic Coasts of Tropical America 121, 158
Fitzgerald, Scott 65, 74, 87, 121, 134
Floridita 24, 28, 30, 30, 31, 32, 43, 43, 52, 122, 148, 149, 149, 155, 157, 160, 161, 161, 162
Flynn, Errol 28, 32, 34, 43, 95, 149, 156
Fogel, Jean-François 41
For Whom the Bell Tolls 12, 52, 57, 58, 86, 121, 122, 126, 129, 132, 137, 142, 161
Fra Angelico 82
Franklyn, Sidney 77
Fuentes, Georgorio 106, 110, 112, 114, 116, 122, 127, 128, 129, 153, 153, 162, 163

García Lorca, Federico 9, 38, 157, 159
García Márquez, Gabriel 23, 34, 40, 148
Gardner, Ava 61, 70, 77, 86, 95, 101, 124, 134, 156
Garibaldi, Giuseppe 65
Gary, Romain 65
Gattorno, Antonio 71, 72, 86, 156
Gaylord's (hotel) 84
Gellhorn, Martha 38, 40, 43, 54, 57, 57, 58, 74, 88, 94, 127, 132, 133, 134, 163
Gide, André 66
Gil Blas de Santillane 65
Gingrich, Arnold 19, 86, 106
Goodman, Benny 64
Gordon, Richard 24
Gould, Morton 64
Goya, Fransisco de 70, 71
Grau San Martín, Ramón 34
Greene, Graham 40, 43, 53, 157, 157
Grelier, Joseph 150, 152
Grey, Zane 138
Gris, Juan 70
Guarida 161
Guest, Winston 129
Guggenheim, Harry E. 40, 43
Guía de la Ciudad Habana 156
Guía provincial de La Habana 22
Guías Social de La Habana 46, 158
Guillén, Nicolás 34, 148, 159
Guiteras, Antonio 35
Gulf Stream 10, 18, 22, 103, 107, 110, 113, 116, 127, 137, 160
Gutiérrez, Carlos 117
Habana Antigua 158
Habana Biltmore 160
Habana-Madrid 43, 138, 139
Hall, Grace 101
Halliburton, Richard 126
Harling, Robert 58
Heart of Darkness 126
Hemingway 12, 19, 74, 78, 94, 95, 107, 122, 132, 138
Hemingway in Cuba 35, 158
Hemingway et son univers 137
Hemingway retrouvé 163
Hemingway, Clarence Edmunds 101
Hemingway, Gregory H. 31, 48, 64, 66, 71, 78, 85, 114, 124, 128, 136, 137
Hemingway, histoire d'une vie 10
Hemingway, My Brother 22, 31, 88, 90, 116, 117, 133
Hemingway, Patrick 52, 64, 66, 71, 139
Hemingway, Pauline 9, 94
Herrera, Roberto 28, 84, 116
Hickock, Guy 19
Holiday 120, 127, 161
Hortons Bay 102
Hostal Valencia 156, 157
Hotchner, A. E. 14, 18, 28, 49, 54, 57, 71, 88, 96, 101, 123, 136, 137

Hotel Almendares 30
Hotel Ambos Mundos 24, 30, 31, 36, 37, 38, 43, 49, 57, 103, 148, 148, 153, 155, 157, 157
Hotel Capri 36
Hotel Comodoro 36
Hotel de Mme Pebaite 153
Hotel Deauville 36
Hotel Havana Hilton 36, 46
Hotel Inglaterra 30, 148, 156, 157, 161
Hotel Nacional 22, 36, 48, 156, 157, 161, 162
Hotel Plaza 156, 157
Hotel Santa Isabel 155
Hotel Sevilla 148, 151, 156, 157, 157, 161
Hotel Sevilla-Biltmore 15, 24, 30
House of Lezama Lima 148
How it was 90, 91
How Young to Look 65
Hudson, Thomas 30, 43, 71, 74, 95, 97, 107, 123, 126 , 128, 129, 137, 153, 155, 160
Hughes, Langston 34
Hynckes, Paul R. 70
Ibarlucia, Fransisco 129
International Fishing Club 144
Islands in the Stream 10, 12, 24, 30, 31, 34, 36, 43, 58, 61, 74, 95, 96, 103, 123, 126, 128, 129, 129, 137, 142, 151, 153, 155, 159
In Peace as in War 48
Interviews et déclarations 9
Ivancich, Adriana 47, 94, 95, 97
Izquierdo Funcia, Claudio 158
Jaimanitas 117, 160
Jordan, Robert 126, 161
Journal d'un salaud 66
Kachkine, Ivan 54
Kane, Bob 156
Kansas City Times 82
Kern, Gerome 64
Ketchum 52, 97, 136, 142
Key West 10, 11, 12, 18, 19, 22, 23, 24, 57, 70, 87, 103, 110, 116, 117, 163
Key West: An Island Sheaf 151
Kinnan Rawlings, Marjorie 14
Kipling, Rudyard 80
Klee, Paul 61, 70
Knapp, Joseph 116
La bodeguita del medio 149
La Colline de l'Ange 156
Ladies on the banks of the river 72
La Divina Pastora 148
The Farm 64, 66, 70, 96
La Force de l'âge 52
La Habana Elegante 160
La Habana Vieja 15, 19, 22, 24, 25, 28, 42, 147, 149, 153, 155, 156, 157, 159
La pesca de la aguja en las costas de Cuba 103

La Peste 138
La Pina de Plata 149
La Poesía Moderna 30, 43
La Rampa 44
La Regla 9, 10,12, 22, 153, 163, 163
La Terraza 35, 107, 110, 126, 127, 128, 129, 153
La Tour Blanche 95
La Zaragonzana 24
Lamparilla (street) 40
Lanham, Charles T. (General) 54, 98, 122
Lania, Leo 78
Lansky, Meyer 35, 38, 48
Las Ángeles 153
Le FBI et les écrivains 136
Le Torero 70
Leeds, Bill 126
Leicester 22, 31, 65, 90, 116, 133
Les Cahiers d'Art 71
Letter from Havana 44
Lezama Lima, José 44, 46, 55, 154, 156
Librería Cervantes 157
London Sunday Times 99
Look 90, 94
López Serrano, José 157
Luciano, Lucky 35, 48
Lyons, Leonnard 112
Machado, Gerardo (General) 31, 34, 40, 43, 84
Machlin, Milt 88, 162
MacLeish (family) 12
MacLeish, Archibald 83, 116
Madox Ford, Ford 65
Mailer, Norman 123, 134
Malecón (quarter) 22, 23, 24, 44, 46, 52, 148, 156, 157, 158, 161
Malraux, André 144
Manet, Edouardo 148
Manhunt 34
Mannige, Robert 68
Manning, Robert 139, 142 , 149
Manolo Asper (Hotel) 57
Mantagena 82
Marcia Menocal, Mario 28, 84
Marciano, Rocky 95
Marina Hemingway 160
Marianao (quarter) 34, 150
Marquesas (islands) 18
Martí, José 149, 151
Martínez de Campo 155
Martínez, Ángel 148
Mason, Jane 36
Masson, André 70
Mathews, Herbert 137
Matíc, Dusan 134
Matisse, Henri 70
McGraw, John J. 35, 150
Médicis, Laurent de 98
Mellow, James R. 52, 95, 132, 138
Mémoires 34
Memorial "Gramma" 156

Mésaventures du Paradis 40
Mexican Cancionero 64
Meyers, Jeffrey 19, 22, 74, 94, 107, 122
Meza, Ramón 160
Mikoïan, Anastas 52
Miller, Arthur 136
Mirador 148
Miramar 46, 147, 158, 158
Miramar Yatch Club 160
Miró, Joan 64, 66, 70, 71, 96
Moderna Poesía (bookshop) 31, 157
Monument en Arbeit 61
Monumenti della Civilita pittorica italiano 70
Monumento a los Estudiantes de Medicina 156
Monumento al General Máximo Gómez 156
Morand, Paul 9, 32, 34, 66, 157, 157
Moré, Beny 43, 148, 150, 159
Morgan, Harry 22, 34
Morgan, Henry 10, 22
Morro 19, 22, 25, 31, 101, 122, 142
Moveable Feast 12, 24, 61, 96, 97
Mowrer, Hadley 136
Murphy (family) 12
Museum of Old Cars 148
Musée historique municipal de Guanabacoa 163
Museo Carpentier 153
Museo de Arte Colonial 153
Museo de Ciencias Felipe-Poey 160
Museo de la Ciudad 155
Museo de la Revolución 156
Museo de Plata 153
Museo Ernest-Hemingway 163
Museo Nacional de Bellas Artes 156
Mussolini 132
New York Book review 80, 112
New York Herald Tribune 77, 83
New York Post 87, 112
New Yorker 71, 76, 121
Ngaje Ngái (house of the god) 57, 69
No-one Ever Dies 163
Normandie 70, 77
Nuevitas (archipel) 151
Numismatic Museum 148, 148
O'Donnell, Leopoldo (General) 101
O'Reilly 24, 30, 44, 153, 155, 157
Oak Park 101, 122, 136
Obispo (rue) 28, 30, 34, 36, 43, 44, 58, 153, 154, 155, 157
Ordoñez, Antonio 86
Orita (boat) 9, 10Orsenna, Erik 40, 43
Our Man in Havana 40, 46, 53, 157
Palacio de Artesanía 159
Palacio de los Capitanes Generales 44, 155, 155
Palacio de los Condes de Casa Bayona 153
Palacio de los Condes de Santovenía 155

Palacio de los Deportes 24
Palacio de los marqueres de Arcos 153
Palacio de Segundo Cabo 155
Palacio del Conde Lombillo 153
Paladar Estrela 161
Papa Hemingway 14, 28, 49, 57, 84, 85, 86, 88, 101, 123, 124
Paradiso 154, 157
Parque Central 24, 155
Pastor, Juan 97, 148, 163, 163
Paz, Octavio 126
Pelaez, Amelia 44
Pereda, Prudencio de 86
Perez Galdos, Benito 65
Perkins, Max 12
Pfeiffer, Pauline 10, 57, 58, 71
Pierce, Waldo 12, 18, 70, 86
Pilar (boat) 12, 19, 22, 49, 86, 100, 102, 106, 106, 107, 107, 114, 116, 117, 120, 121, 122, 127, 127, 128, 129 , 136, 142, 143, 144, 153, 160, 160, 162, 162, 163
Playas del Este 160
Plaza de Armas 28, 30, 43, 44, 153, 155, 155, 157
Plaza de la Catedral 28, 153, 153
Plaza de la Fuente 24
Plimpton, George 65
Portocarrero, René 44
Portrait of a Woman 71
Pound, Ezra 65, 78, 133, 134
Prado (museum) 71, 156
Prío, Carlos 47, 49
Quintanilla, Luis 71, 86
Reed, John 70, 134
Rhapsodie cubaine 148
Río Luyano 58, 162
Ritz 77, 124
Rancho's 24
Richardson, Hadley 94
Robins, Natalie 136
Rockfeller (family) 34
Rodríguez Feo, José 44
Rolland, Romain 14
Roosevelt, Eleanor 65, 134
Russell, Joe 14, 19, 22, 110, 116, 127
Sabana-Camagüey (archipelago) 151
Saint Louis Star-Times 77
Sálon Copa 150
San Cristobal de La Habana 24
San Fransisco de Paula 48, 58, 58, 59, 67, 97, 98, 142, 153, 162, 162, 163
San Ignacio 24
San Isidro 24
San Rafael 30, 34
Sanchez, Thowald 84
Sans-Souci 36, 150
Santa Cruz del Norte 116
Santiago de Cuba de la Sierra 48
Santísima Virgen de Regla 163, 163

Sarto, Andrea del 71
Sartre, Jean-Paul 54, 86, 95
Saviers, George 96, 97
Saxon, John 129
Seguí, Gilberto 46, 47
Selected Letters 9, 28, 31, 52, 71, 76, 87, 96, 98, 112, 123, 124, 126, 132, 136, 139, 144
Shakespeare and the Dyer's Hand 65
Shangai 40, 161
Shipman, Evan 12, 14
Sinatra, Frank 48, 134, 156
Singer, Kurt 121, 124
Sirena 148
Slopy Joe's 10, 14, 24, 148, 156
Soldevilla, Carlos 160
Stade du Cerro 46, 149, 150
Stein, Gertrude 65, 70, 78, 134
Steward, Don 87
Stork Club 43
Strater, Mike 14
Suerte de Baras 70
Sullivan, Jim 14
Templete 155
Tennessee 30
Test Pilot 65
The big Two Hearted River 103
The Common Reader 65
The Dangerous Summer 12, 49
The Farm 64, 66, 70, 96
The Fisherman's Handbook 65
The Garden of Eden 12, 24, 61
The Good Life 10
The Guitar Player 70The Havana Country Club 150
The Havana General Guide 31, 34, 139
The Killers 35
The Nick Adams Stories 11, 24, 71, 78, 103
The Old Man and the Sea 12, 22, 23, 34, 47, 94, 97, 103, 107, 117, 121, 124, 126, 126, 137, 138, 143, 144, 149, 150, 151, 153, 160
The Paris Review 66, 69, 71, 74, 147
The Pirates'Club 150
The Republic 65
The Roots of heaven 65
The Snows of Kilimanjaro 69, 87, 138
The Stricken Field 57
The Sun Also Rises 12
The Tradesman's return 22,
Théâtre Blanquita 43
Théâtre Nacional 40, 44
Thomas, John Charles 12
Thomson, Charles 14
Times 52, 80
To Have and Have Not 10, 12, 22, 24, 34, 36, 151
Toronto Daily Star 103
Toronto Star Weekly 103
Torre y Huerta, Carlos de la 121, 158

Trinidad Colonial 161
Three Sad Tigers 46, 147, 150
Tropicana 40, 48, 150, 150
Twain, Mark 103, 120
Tynan, Kenneth 52, 161
Un personaje llamado Hemingway 158
USA or Manhattan Transfer 11
Valdès, Zoé 8, 29, 55
Varadero 35, 150
Vedado 44, 46, 47, 52, 53, 138, 147, 156, 157, 158
Veloso Guerra, Ricardo 157
Verdun 65
Villareal, René 90
Villaverde, Cirilo 156
Walden, Harry 87
Walsh, Rodolfo 52
Washington Post 121
Waugh, Evelyn 137
Welsh, Mary 24, 47, 57, 60, 61, 62, 64, 66, 71, 73, 74, 82, 83, 85, 89, 90, 90, 91, 94, 95, 95, 96, 97, 99, 106, 126, 136, 142, 151, 159, 162, 163
Wheeler Shipyard 106, 121
Whitehead Street 11
Williams, Kenneth 30
Williams, Tennessee 28
Wolfe, Tom 121
Wood, Peggy 65
Woolf, Virginia 65
Young, Philip 88

Credits

© Museo Ernest Hemingway, Finca Vigía, all rights reserved, photographs by Jean-Bernard Naudin: pp. 6, 30(bottom), 40, 57(top), 64(bottom), 66(bottom), 68(top), 70(top), 74, 78(bottom), 80(top, left), 86(top), 88, 94, 97(top), 98(bottom), 101(top), 102, 106(top), 112, 120, 129(top), 132(top), 134, 136(top and bottom), 137, 153(bottom), 160(top).
© Antonio Gattorno/All rights reserved: p. 72
© A. Parinet: p. 72.

Acknowledgements

I would like to thank all those who helped me produce this book: Daniel Nees; Chantal Bruel, Brigitte Benderriter, Hélène de Saint-Hypolite; Edouardo Manet, Philipe Ollé-Laprune; Laurence Basset, Cécile Aoustin, Sabine Büchsenschütz from Editions du Chêne; La Chica del museo, and Patricia Reznikov.

GÉRARD DE CORTANZE

My warmest thanks go to Jean Baudot, who organized our trip, Raunda Jamis for her helpful advice and Françoise Dubois-Sigmund. Over in Havana, thanks also to Gladys Rodriguez-Ferrero, Curator of the Hemingway Museum, Noël Adrian and Laurent Pillet from Havana Club International, Gustavo Di Meza-Perez, Manager of the Floridita, Gregorio Fuentes, one of the oldest people to have known Hemingway, and our chauffeur Fédérico, all of whom were extremely helpful.

JEAN-BERNARD NAUDIN

Editions du Chêne would also like to thank Groupe Accor and the Hotel Coralia Sévilla in Havana.
This book was produced with the help of AOM.

EDITORIAL MANAGER
Laurence Basset

ASSISTED BY
Cécile Aoustin

LAYOUT
Sabine Büchsenschütz

Production
L'Atelier Helzevir, Maisons-Alfort
Photo Engraving
Offset Publicité, Maisons-Alfort

Binding : AGM, à Forges-les-Eaux
Printed in France by Clerc,
Saint-Amand-Montrond
Resgistration : 4129-septembre 1997
ISBN : 2.84.277326-8

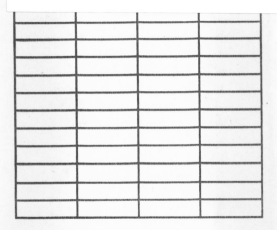

CUBA

OCEANO ATLANTICO – MAR CARIBE

ESCALA: 1: 1 000 000 (25°00')

Profundidades en metros
Alturas en metros
Sistema de Balizamiento Marítimo IALA–Región B
Rojo a estribor (Red to Starboard)
Fuentes: Carta cubana 1001 con correcciones posteriores

Curvas de Variación Magnética para 1990
La variación magnética se muestra en gráfica seguida por las letras E–W, según corresponda (adjunto a la curva). El cambio anual está expresado en minutos con la letra E o W y se dá entre paréntesis inmediatamente seguido de la variación.

DISPOSITIVOS DE SEPARACION DE TRAFICO
Todos los Dispositivos de Separación de Tráfico cartografiados en las inmediaciones de la República de Cuba han sido adoptados por la OMI. Los mismos fueron puestos en vigor desde el 1 de junio de 1989 y se encuentran listados en el Apéndice III del RIPA (P–9401) editado en 1992. Para más información remitase a cartas de escalas mayores.